THE MACHIAVELLIAN'S GUIDE TO WOMANIZING

The Machiavellian's Guide to Womanizing

Nick Casanova

CASTLE BOOKS

This edition published by Castle Books,
a division of Book Sales, Inc.
114 Northfield Avenue
Edison, NJ 08837
1999
Published by arrangement with and permission of
Carroll & Graf Publishers, Inc.
260 Fifth Avenue
New York, NY 10001

ISBN 0-7858-1074-9
Printed in the United States of America

To G.H., whose sterling character and many war stories provided the moral framework for this scholarly tome.

Acknowledgments

This book would not have been possible without the inspiration of all the women who ever rejected me and sent me off on these flights of fancy.

Contents

Introduction

In the sixteenth century, Niccolò Machiavelli wrote a book, *The Prince*, about how to gain and keep political power through devious means. He has since received more than his fair share of vilification. In the popular mind, Machiavelli's name has become synonymous with duplicity and evil. Whether this is justified is debatable. What is beyond debate is that those who have followed his teachings in the intervening centuries have met with great success.

Had Machiavelli focused his energies on womanizing, this is the book he would have written.

Women who talk about a man who knows "every trick in the book" are referring to this book. Herein are successful strategies in the war between the sexes. This book is not so much an outlining of the rules of the game as an underlining that there are not rules. (In seduction, it's not how you play the game, it's whether you win or lose).

There's not need for guilt. Women are Machiavellian, too. The only difference is that with them it's called "using their feminine wiles." This book will help you develop your masculine wiles.

People say that all's fair in love and war, the point of which is that everything in love is unfair. If you'd prefer the unfairness at your enemy's expense, this book is for you.

THE MACHIAVELLIAN'S GUIDE
TO WOMANIZING

The List

The wish to acquire is admittedly a very natural and common thing; and when men succeed in this they are always praised rather than condemned.

—Niccolò Machiavelli

Popular wisdom has it that the career womanizer is only in love with himself. Actually, he is in love with his list.

Most guys keep a list, tucked safely away in a bottom drawer, of the women they've scored with. (Many women keep similar tallies.) How many on your list?

0–10 This book is worth its weight in gold to you.
11–20 You can obviously use our help.
21–30 This book will help perfect your style.
31–50 Many chapters will have a familiar ring to you.
  50+ Your help is needed with the second edition.

The most important thing about your list is never, ever to let a woman know you keep it. If she finds out, she will do everything in her power to keep herself off it. If a woman ever asks you how many women you've slept with, maintain you've only slept with four. Round the number down rather than up, the way you do when one of the guys ask.

The message you must convey is that you care more about

1

quality than quantity, even though the opposite is true. If you must mention your list, make sure it's only after she's on it.

One thing all lists have in common no matter how many names they boast is that there's always room for more.

Are You a Hound?

Is this book for you? To find out, take this simple test: Would you rather spend ten nights making love to the same beautiful woman, or a night each with ten different beautiful women?

If you would rather spend all ten nights with one woman, read no further.

But if you're like most guys, you chose ten different women. This means, whether you realize it or not, that at heart you are a hound. Don't struggle against it—four million years of human evolution have molded you to be this way. In fact, the only real perversity would be to rebel against these instincts.

When you get tired of a woman after a couple of weekends, it is because thousands of generations of your ancestors are in effect urging you to spread your sperm (i.e., your genes) more widely. Don't disappoint them. Let variety be the spice of your sex life.

Women have been selected over millions of years of evolution to have different mating instincts, most of which boil down to selecting a mate who has good genes, who will stay with them, and who will be a good provider. Thus, from the dawn of history, they have fallen for a certain type of guy—the type this book will help you pretend to be.

Politics and fashions change from year to year but basic human instincts would take hundreds of generations to change. So whatever the current status of feminism and sexual politics, rest assured that this book is quite timely.

Part I
Tactics

The Big Lie

Princes who have achieved great things have been those who have given their word lightly, who have known how to trick men with their cunning, and who, in the end, have overcome those abiding by honest principles.

—Niccolò Machiavelli

Most women prefer to think that seduction is a matter of two people who have a lot in common being overwhelmed by the passion of the moment rather than a well-orchestrated attack. And every woman instantly raises her guard against a guy on the make. (For some reason women are unable to accept being just another notch on your bedpost.)

So play along with the Big Lie. Pretend sex is the furthest thing from your mind. Offhand comments such as: "People pay so much attention to sex. It's just not that big a deal" show that friendship is the only thing on your mind. (It also makes you sound more experienced.) "I used to be into one-night stands, but I've outgrown those" also shows that your heart's in the right place.

Don't ever say, "I just want to have a good time." Most women know that translates directly as "To me, you're only a lay." And no woman is susceptible to "Come on—I'm in the middle of a hot streak, so don't ruin it."

Voice your distasteful reaction to singles bars ("They're just *meat* markets!") and recite the Sensitive Person's Pledge of Allegiance ("I could *never* go to bed with someone I didn't care about.").

The hard part is looking sincere while you utter these insincerities."

Sixteen Comments That Show You're a Sensitive Guy

It is not necessary for a prince to have the above-mentioned qualities, but it is very necessary to seem to have them.
—Niccolò Machiavelli

If your prospective target likes warmth, caring, and sensitivity on the part of a lover, and you have her fooled so far, these lines will confirm that you're Mr. Right:

- I'm not ashamed to admit it. I've cried plenty of times.
- Boxing should be abolished.
- You know, it's funny, but I usually get along better with women than I do with men.
- Did you see the sunset yesterday evening? Wow!
- I can't stand big apartment buildings. I want to live in a house with a garden.
- I have a lot of gay friends.
- I *love* children. And the amazing thing is—there's so much you can learn from them.
- That's such a beautiful dog/cat/painting/whatever she has in her apartment.
- I bake my own bread.
- I'm a charter member of ASPCA/Greenpeace/The Sierra Club.

- I really don't care what a woman looks like, as long as her inner beauty shines through.
- If I seem a little reluctant to become involved too quickly, it's because once, a long time ago, someone hurt me very deeply.
- You really don't appreciate your parents until you leave home.
- Zoos are so inhuman. Animals weren't meant to be cooped up.
- I may look tough on the outside, but on the inside I'm just a frightened Mama's boy.
- I spent a year working with retarded people. It really helped me grow.

These comments are more effective when used in context; but if you can't, just drop them anywhere.

If your prospect likes her men macho, simply reverse the above statements ("They oughta just take all the retards out and shoot them").

How to Sound Sincere

Telling a woman what she wants to hear generally means telling her how much you like her. There are many ways of expressing affection. Some are hokey ("I would give the sun, the moon, and the stars for you, were they but mine to give"); some are weak ("I don't *dislike* you"); some don't make any sense ("I worship the very ground you walk on"); and some are obviously untrue ("I'm happy if you're happy").

9

The following lines, in order of ascending affection, are to be uttered at increasingly familiar stages of the relationship. They sound spontaneous and therefore sincere.

- You know something? You're really good company. I mean *really* good.
- That was the first really enjoyable date I've been on in a long time.
- You know, I like you more than I've ever liked any girl after just two dates.
- I hope we're friends for a long, long time.
- I've noticed something funny recently . . . I'm always happy when I'm with you.
- I'm so glad I met you. It scares me to think, if I hadn't happened to need directions on that street corner that day . . .
- This sounds trite, but I feel so close to you. It's as if I've known you for a lot longer than just three weeks.
- You're one of the nicest girls I've ever met . . . the kind I'd want to . . . well . . . (At this point look away as if you said something you hadn't intended to let slip.).
- I can't imagine ever changing the way I feel about you.
- I can't think of anyone else I'd rather spend the rest of my life with. (This comes perilously close to proposing.)

You can always resort to "I love you," but this has become a bit of a cliché.

Propose Marriage

A prince . . . must learn how not to be virtuous, and to make use of this or not according to need.
—Niccolò Machiavelli

"Never tell a woman you love her, even if you do" is the conventional wisdom. However, implying it strongly can sometimes help you storm the citadel. The best way to do this? Propose marriage. Very few women don't let their defenses down when proposed to. (If the woman actually accepts, it can be sticky extricating yourself.) If your target has you pegged as a womanizer, proposing will defuse her suspicion. And if she is seriously weighing your offer, she'll have the incentive to take a test drive.

If you think she'll doubt your sincerity, don't propose on your first date. A dozen red roses should prove your intent; while they will run upward of fifty dollars, the satisfaction is, if not guaranteed, certainly much more likely. A fake diamond engagement ring, available in any five-and-dime store, is another useful prop.

You probably don't propose every day, so a few rehearsals are helpful. Erupting into laughter while asking for her hand will diminish your matrimonial credibility. If you can't bring yourself to propose, at least hint strongly that you're interested in getting married. This will get her antennae up.

11

Then, when describing the qualities you're looking for in a wife, list hers.

Don't actually get married. The idea may seem vaguely appealing, especially if you haven't worshiped at her altar yet, but remember, eternal vigilance is the price of liberty.

Flattery

Women love flattery—and the less they deserve it, the more grateful they are. Just don't make it too unbelievable or they'll think you're mocking them. Flattery, like humor, works best when it contains a grain of truth.

But don't go to the other extreme. Unvarnished honesty will only backfire, such as: "You must look great when you're wearing makeup"; "Sometimes, when you're quiet, I almost like you"; or "If you just lost twenty-five pounds, you'd be gorgeous."

Ask permission to take her picture. Women either love or hate to have their picture taken: either way, they're flattered to be asked. If she's got a sense of humor, ask, "May I take your picture? I need something to jerk off over."

Ask, "You're not related to (a certain movie star), are you?" If you see the slightest resemblance, be it ever so faint, rest assured she will have already seen it. People always think they resemble a better-looking version of themselves, and your target will undoubtedly be pleased that somebody else spotted the resemblance.

One effective way to flatter her is to praise her to her best friend. This friend will undoubtedly repeat your compliments to your target. Your target should be delighted to hear this. (The sincerity of a compliment delivered to one's face is always suspect, but compliments behind one's back are generally considered to be meant.)

Go ahead and whisper those sweet nothings into her ear, even if that's all they are.

Nine Ways to Tell a Woman She's Beautiful

"Gee, you're looking beautiful" is not unpleasant for any woman to hear, but it sounds like a compliment a father might give. Here are some lines to make her swoon.

—It's really unfair that most women are sort of ordinary-looking and a few get to look like you.
—All four of your grandparents must have been very good-looking to produce someone as drop-dead gorgeous as you.
—I'll bet you've broken a lot of hearts with that face of yours.
—No one could have a face that perfect without plastic surgery. (You're risking that she's had it.)
—Every now and then Mother Nature just takes it upon herself to create a masterpiece.
—You're one of the three best-looking women I've ever seen. (Be prepared to name the other two.)

13

—I never thought I'd see a girl with a perfect face *and* a perfect body. Occasionally you see one or the other, but never both.
—Helen of Troy must have looked something like you.
—The amazing thing about your face is it doesn't have a single flaw! (If she points one out, say, "No! That just makes you more beautiful.")

These lines work best with a woman whose looks rate a natural six or seven on a scale of ten and through dieting and makeup has made herself a seven or eight. If the woman is a nine or a ten, she'll have heard similar flattery before and will remain unaffected. If she's below a six, she'll think you're mocking her.

Be a Good Listener

One of the oldest jokes around is that so-and-so's best quality is that he's a "good listener." However, since most people's favorite subject *is* by far themselves, to give a woman a truly enjoyable date, be prepared to let her discuss her favorite subject all evening long. (The emphasis is on long.)

Most people—and men are equally guilty of this—define "getting to know you" as telling you all about themselves. The difference between men and women is that women consider this a prerequisite for sex. So act as if she has your undivided attention while she spews out banal details about her friends, her family, her job, her co-workers, her favorite movie stars, et cetera. Profess admiration, approval, astonishment, and sympathy when each is called for.

Should you find your attention wandering, remember that all that is really required to keep up appearances is a few nods of the head and an occasional repeating of her last few words with a questioning tone.

At some point, she may begin to feel self-conscious about having blabbed on, and will ask you about yourself. You need only say, "Oh, my life isn't nearly as interesting as yours. I just work in a boring office every day." Then ask her to elaborate on some aspect of her life, sit back, and try not to look bored.

Listen to her talk long enough, and you may get to hear her moan later on.

Show You're a Nice Guy

Above all else, a woman who's checking you out cares about whether you're a nice guy. There are easier ways to do this than act like a saint all the time. The easiest way is to talk about your volunteer work. (And be sure to pooh-pooh it afterward.)

"Saturday afternoons I work for the ASPCA uptown." After she remarks on how nice you are for doing it, say, "I'm not doing it because I'm nice, I do it 'cause it makes me feel good."

*   *   *

"I think everybody should give a tenth of their income to charity. I do." (Be prepared to list your charities.)

"Once, when I was working at a gym, I saw this old wino outside, so I asked him to come in and take a shower. That poor guy hadn't showered in ages." (The implication is if you treat a bum that well, you'll treat her at least as well.)

"I worked for the Peace Corps in Ethiopia for a year after college. It was frustrating not being able to help those people any more than I could. One year was all I could take."

This technique is most effective when demonstrated first-hand. When you and your date walk by an indigent person, hand him a five (it'll be worth it) and tell him, trying to sound as concerned as you can, "Don't spend it on booze. Buy yourself a sandwich or something." Try not to look pleased with yourself (the kiss of death for any would-be saint).

She may be touched enough by your kindness and generosity to let you touch her later on.

Act Dazzled By Her Looks

If a woman is not secure about her attractiveness, (i.e., if she is a woman), you can often ingratiate yourself with an indirect form of flattery.

You meet a woman, start a conversation, and find she is

interested in, say, meditation. You express a desire to try it, though you haven't the least interest, and get her phone number. A few days later you call and say, "Hi, this is Nick. I'm the fellow who was asking you about meditation the other day." After your target says hello, admit, "I have to confess, I'm masquerading under false pretenses. I told you I'm interested in meditation, and I am, vaguely, but the truth is, mostly I just wanted to stare at you. How about I just buy you a drink instead."

You'll get a positive response for three reasons. First, she will have suspected that your interest in meditation was only a ploy to begin with, and your admission makes you seem honest. Second, your confession makes you out to be the type who can admit fault, always a good sign. Third, of course, is the sheer flattery value of your statement.

When you meet her, carry on a casual conversation, and don't refer to her looks directly. Then, the first time you make a verbal blunder, shake your head and say, "Being around a woman who looks like you has always turned me into a blithering idiot."

Indirect flattery comes across as more sincere because it seems less calculated. After all, you didn't intend to stumble over your words. That the excuse flatters her seems almost accidental.

At some point offer, "I'm *trying* to judge you on the merits of your conversation. I have to keep reminding myself, beauty is only skin deep."

Flattery can be most effective when it approaches your target from an oblique angle.

The Pass

Few things are more embarrassing than an awkward pass. It doesn't help that the woman usually seems able to sense them coming.

One way to avoid this embarrassment is to be humorous: "If you don't get up from this couch by the time I count to three, I'm going to kiss you." Before she can move, quickly count to three. If she rebuffs your advances, it will be more as if you made a joke than a pass, and you won't have to feel foolish.

Or say, "I have a secret to tell you." This is your excuse to lean in close. Then whisper in her ear, "I find you very attractive." It's much easier to kiss her from this position than it is to lunge in her direction and aggressively thrust your face at hers.

But the best way to make contact is not to appear to be making a pass at all. Calmly ask, "Will you do me a big favor?"

"What's that?"

"Give me a hug."

This sounds as if all you want is a little affection, and it's hard for her flatly to say no. Once she's in your arms, it's much easier to progress to a kiss, partly because it's harder for her to break away, but also because she will be touched by this evidence of your warmth. And the mere fact that she's returned your hug will help disperse her own inhibitions. In fact, when you draw away slightly after you hug, while your face is still close to hers, the natural inclination for both of you will be to kiss. If you resist the impulse, chances are *she* will go ahead and kiss *you*—so in a sense *she* will be the one making the pass. If you're feeling playful, pull your head back and say, "Did I give you permission to kiss me?"

One secret to making a pass is to be perfectly still, just like a statue, beforehand. For some inexplicable reason, this seems to have a hypnotic effect on women. Try it. You'll be surprised.

These instructions, followed explicitly, will enable you to hit pay dirt with much greater regularity.

The Massage

Most women love massages; more importantly, they're more acquiescent after receiving one. The only problem is convincing them beforehand that your intentions stop there.

Never ask, "Can I give you a massage?" This places the burden of acceptance on her. Just say, "Lie down on your stomach, I know how to relax you." If she demurs, answer firmly, "Don't be silly. I'm just going to rub your back."

One line of attack is, "If you don't trust me, you don't have to accept one, but my back is really killing me, so could you give me one?" If you're on superficially good terms, she can hardly turn you down. Extend the massage as long as you can, and grunt appreciatively at frequent intervals. At some point murmur, "I swear, I like massages better than sex." This will remind her how nice a massage is, and also make you seem less of a sex fiend. If she doesn't want to be paid back for fairness' sake, she'll probably need a massage after all the time she's spent bent over you.

If this fails, tell her that you are a licensed masseur. Most women have always wanted to receive a professional massage but haven't either because of the illicit implications or because it seems extravagant to pay twenty dollars for a half-hour massage. (A massage table in your apartment can be an invaluable prop.).

Once your hands have started to work their hypnotic magic, it is a simple matter to remove her clothing piece by piece. It helps to reassure her (e.g., "I'm just untucking your blouse so I can do your lower back better"; "I'm just un-hooking this clasp because it's in the way"). By this point, she should be enjoying the massage so much that she won't object.

Still, it's important not to show unseemly haste in getting at those hard-to-get-to places.

Telltale Signs

Unfortunately, no one has yet invented the machine that, when held up to a woman in the manner of a Geiger counter, will tell you whether she is willing to go to bed with you. So until someone invents the pussy meter, you will have to rely on the many clues that women drop, knowingly and unknowingly.

Good Signs	_Bad Signs_
Patting her hair or adjusting her nylons upon seeing you.	Taking out her compact and freshening her makeup in front of you.
Looking at you frequently.	Frequently consulting her watch.
Acting flirtatious with you.	Acting flirtatious with other men.
Leaning back and stretching (showing her breasts to best effect).	Crossing her arms and legs.
Laughing at all your jokes.	Pretending not to hear your jokes.
Comparing you favorably with her ex-boyfriend.	Comparing you unfavorably with her ex-boyfriend.
Beating out a drumroll on her thighs, or hips.	Drumming her fingernails on the tabletop.
Telling you she's got a great little apartment.	Telling you her apartment is a mess.
"Give me a call."	"I'll call you."

Too many bad signs means it's time to cut your losses. Walking out in the middle of dinner is bit abrupt—but at least you won't waste any more time that way.

How to Translate Her Words

While you must devote much attention to how women will interpret your words, you ought not to ignore the fact that females are also quite capable of double-talk (at times it seems that's the only talk they're capable of).

When She Says	*She Means*
I'm not ready for a heavy relationship right now.	I'm just not ready for a heavy relationship with you right now.
Oh, God, I'm so tired this evening.	You better not be expecting sex tonight.
I'm underpaid at my job.	I hope you're picking up the tab.
I don't understand how some people can have sex with someone they barely know.	If you want *this* pussy, you better settle in for a *long* siege.
Describe your ideal woman.	Describe me.
We're going to have *lots of time* to see each other.	We'll be seeing each other *lots of times* before I let you fuck me.
Oh, I'm so unattractive.	Tell me I'm beautiful.

My last boyfriend was incredibly cheap.	You're going to have to spend two hundred bucks up front, *minimum*, before you get in *here*.
I love you.	Tell me you love me.

Going on a date is often like taking an intensive Berlitz lesson in female double-talk. (Some women are so patently transparent that no translation lessons are necessary.)

How to Tell if She's Interested

There are many standard clues that women drop, knowingly and unknowingly.

Does she looks at you a lot? If you catch her staring at you more than three times, she wants you. (Naturally, this assumes you're not engaged in any outrageous behavior that merits gawking.) Think about it. Do you stare at women you want? Yes. Do you stare at women you don't want? No. Women are less visual, but they are not blind.

If she asks about your family, she's interested. (She wouldn't bother if she didn't care.) Of course, if she keeps asking about your older brother, she's probably more interested in him.

If she asks about your likes and dislikes, she's prospecting for future activities for the two of you.

If she says you're "interesting," she's interested.

If she laughs at all your jokes, even the lame ones, you've got her hooked.

If she asks if you have a girlfriend, it can mean that she's interested. (You must judge from the context—she might just be casually curious about your sexuality.)

If you're not receiving the desired feedback, take the initiative: "There's something that's been bothering me recently, and I have to know." When she asks what's wrong, look very concerned and say, "Do you find me attractive?" She may blurt out something revealing as she laughs.

If it's a woman you've just met, there's one way to judge her interest with no loss of face. Simply say, "You're attractive. If I weren't married, I'd ask you out." If she doesn't respond positively, let the subject drop. She may respond, "Oh, well, if you weren't married, I'd go out with you, too." Reply, "Guess what? I'm not married. What are you doing Friday night?"

She can't turn you down without making a liar of herself.

Banter

Teasing a woman about her appearance is a good way to play on her insecurities, compelling her to prove her attractiveness in ways she might not otherwise—like trying to lure you into bed.

If she has so much as one white hair, ask, "Is that a white hair?" Inquire how old she is, then reply, "Really? Normally when I meet a gray-haired lady, I assume she's much older."

If she protests, chuckle and comment, "you look like you've seen your share of tequila sunrises."

Peer at her closely, then express pleasant surprise: "Oh, you're growing a mustache!" (Every woman is self-conscious about the peach fuzz on her upper lip.)

Suggest, "You should do something about that jawline." Add helpfully, "I know the name of a good doctor."

Try, "Have you put on some weight?" When she denies it, express surprise.

If she makes a joke you've heard before (most jokes fall into this category), reply, "I applaud not only the humor but the originality of your joke." Or just nod politely. She may actually attempt to relate a long joke with a beginning, middle, and end (most women are constitutionally incapable of doing so). After she delivers the punch line, ask, "What happened then?"

If she asks what you think of her new dress, reply, "How much did it cost?" When she tells you, wince.

If she stumbles over her words, immediately retort, "Well put."

If she expresses her opinion on anything, you can reply, "Always have to be the center of attention, don't you."

If she shows any tomboyish tendencies whatsoever, furrow your brow and ask, "Have you ever had a boyfriend?"

Just because you don't end up in bed with a woman doesn't mean you can't have fun at her expense.

Off-Color Banter

Taking flirtation a step further brings you into the realm of sexual insult. Keep in mind that this line of talk will go over only with a certain type of woman—one who is extremely forward and flirtatious herself.

Saying either "I bet you're a real nymphomaniac" or "You seem like the type who'd have a real hard time reaching orgasm" will elicit a strong response from your target.

Ogle other women as they walk by. Remarks such as, "Nice ass, that" or "Whatta set of lungs" set just the right tone for your conversation.

If she lights up a cigarette, comment, "They say women who smoke just love giving blow jobs. Is that true?" If she has an attractive mouth, enthuse, "Those lips were just made for blow jobs."

Gesture at her loin area and say, "Bet there're a few miles on that odometer." If she gets mad, reply, "Hit a sore point, did I?"

If she has a bruise on her leg, comment, "If you have to get it cut off, keep in mind I have a penchant for amputees."

If she's wearing tight pants, marvel. "Those pants are pulled up so tight you must have to have one labia pulled over on one side and the other on the other side."

Muse, "You strike me as the type of woman who spends a lot of her spare time masturbating."

If she expresses dismay at any of your comments, reply,

"What are you getting so hoity-toity about? You're not exactly a vestal virgin."

As long as you're playing the role of bad boy, you might as well play it to the hilt.

Playing Hard to Get

This book is mostly about demonstrating counterfeit affection; but there are times when it is better to do the opposite. If you make yourself too available, you can lose your appeal.

You must judge your quarry correctly: Some women need lots of attention, other prefer a little challenge. (It's a fatal mistake to smother the latter.)

Pretending indifference is easy (and often fun). At the early stages of courtship it can be accomplished simply by forgetting her name or not looking at her very much. (Constantly staring is a dead giveaway that you desire her.)

After you call her by the wrong name, immediately apologize and correct yourself. The desired impression will be left. This mistake becomes increasingly insulting the longer you know her. (For utmost effect, moan the wrong name during sex.)

Ask, "Were you the one who used to ride horses?" This is even more effective than calling her by the wrong name (a mere slip of the tongue), because it means you have her genuinely confused with someone else.

If your relationship has not reached the physical stage yet, share a soft drink with her. Each time before you take a swig, thoroughly wipe off the neck of the bottle where her lips have touched it. (Women being women, she will then want proof you're not put off by close physical contact.)

Standing her up on a date (even if you want to go) can convey the correct attitude. Afterward, don't claim an emergency; tell her you simply forgot about the date (but be profusely apologetic).

Don't act like a doormat and you won't get treated like one.

Show You're Attractive to Other Women

If your date is susceptible to mob psychology, all you need do to brainwash her into falling for you is show how desirable you are to other women. Arrange to have a buddy phone your apartment several times during the course of an evening. Each time you answer the phone, your date should hear something like the following. (Talk secretively, as if you don't want her to hear, but loudly enough for her to get the gist of the conversations.)

"Hi, Sue-Ann ... Fine, thanks ... I'd like to but I promised George I'd help him move. . . . No, there's no one else here. . . . I'll give you a call. . . . Yeah, soon, bye."

"Hi, Yasmine, you caught me just as I was going out the door. . . . I've got to get to my tailor. He closes in five minutes. . . . Okay, tomorrow evening. See you."

"Hi! How's California? Fine. . . . Listen, you caught me at a bad time . . . Mike's over and we're watching the game. . . . Okay, see you at the airport then. . . . Me, too. . . . Love you, bye-bye."

If your date asks who phoned, reply, "Oh, no one." After the third call, unplug the phone and say, "People I haven't heard from in months are coming out of the woodwork tonight." This obvious lie should convince her you're a hot item.

If your date suggests you're quite a ladies' man, deny it repeatedly; this is tantamount to admitting it. By this point she should be keenly aware of what a prize you are and want you herself.

Making Her Jealous

If a woman is taking you for granted, nothing will revitalize her flagging attention like a healthy dose of jealousy.

There are many ways to make a woman jealous. Some are subtle, some not so subtle. When you pass by another nubile young thing in the street, turn around and check out her backside. Then sigh deeply. If you make eye contact with the passerby, smile at her (this is an outright declaration of war).

Anytime you're near a newsstand, pick up a girlie magazine and flip through it. (This can have an off-putting effect on a first date.) Better yet, leave a few skin magazines around your place. Idly pick one up during the course of a conversation and absentmindedly leaf through it.

Ask your girlfriend, "Do you think Susan is pretty?" She'll respond sharply, "No. Why? Do you?" Reply, "Just curious, that's all."

Tell her, "If I wasn't going out with you, I'd go after Becky." She will interpret this to mean that you'd like to go after Becky, which, of course, is what it does mean.

If a well-dressed nymphet sashays by, examine her closely, then comment, "Nice dress." (Heterosexual males never pay attention to a woman's clothes.)

Ask, "Have you ever had an open relationship?" She'll say something like "No. I think that's disgusting. Why? Do you want one?" Reply, "No, of course not, I was just asking, that's all."

If she should have occasion to ask what you were doing on a certain night, quickly answer, "Nothing . . . nothing." (No one ever does absolutely nothing.)

If she decides to counterattack by ogling a few guys, laugh as if you think she's cute. (Nothing makes a woman more insecure than total lack of jealousy on your part.)

Tell her you got a call from an old girlfriend the day before. When your target asks what she wanted, reply, "She wanted to have a drink sometime, that's all. You know, just as friends."

Too much of this behavior can lead to a fight and even a breakup, but in the right dosages it can tie your target into knots of insecurity, which is just how you want her.

If She Asks You Your Sign

As everybody with an IQ in excess of 93 knows, astrology is a preoccupation of the addlebrained. However, if a pretty woman asks your sign, *don't* demonstrate your wisdom by saying "Jeeeesus *Christ*! You don't believe in *that* shit, do you?"

The best reply is simply "Guess," which identifies you as a fellow believer. If she has asked you your sign, there's interest on her part; this means she hopes you're compatible, and therefore she'll pick a compatible sign for you. So when she makes her guess, reply, "That's right! How did you know?" At this point she'll gladly give a long-winded explanation. Feign interest.

Once she's started out believing you're compatible, chances are you *will* be compatible, partly because her attitude will create a self-fulfilling prophecy, and partly because her attitude will create a self-fulfilling prophecy, and partly because avid astrologers constantly look for facts bearing out their predictions. And after all, how many intelligent men (you've already proved *you're* intelligent by reading this book) will listen spellbound while she expounds on how the gravitational pull of the stars when you're born exerts such a profound influence on your later life?

Now, the stars exert less gravitational influence on you during birth than a cigarette lighter in the operating room, and there's as much real science in astrology as there is in the distribution of Chinese fortune cookies at dinner, but if you play along with her game, chances are greater she'll play along with yours.

If You Excel at a Sport

All men are showoffs at heart, and you are no exception. And with good reason. For the last four million years, women have been evolutionarily selected for mating with men who would be good providers. For most of that time, providing entailed running fast and throwing spears accurately. These days one's ability as a provider has precious little to do with one's spear-throwing prowess, but women still succumb to such atavistic charms. However, if you want to demonstrate your athletic skills, there is a way to do it and a way not to do it.

Don't boast about your prowess, then insist she watch you. She'll be less impressed because of her raised expectations. She'll think you a conceited boor. And she'll feel obliged to praise you afterward, an awkward position for anyone.

Let's say you're a good butterflier. Your approach should be something like this: "I'm due for a time trial Saturday. It will be boring for you, but I'd be grateful if you came: Your presence would undoubtedly inspire me to a better performance."

Portray yourself as mediocre befor hand ("I just hope I can finish the four laps"). And rest assured few women know the difference between a good and a bad athletic performance anyway. (Any guy who lifts knows that bench pressing two hundred pounds is commonplace, but few women know that.)

Afterward, your instinct will be to insist what she just witnessed was a subpar performance. It's better to tell her the opposite ("Knowing you were watching took two seconds off my time").

At the same time, profess embarrassment that you participate in your sport ("Pretty mindless way to spend an afternoon, eh?"; "Pathetic, isn't it, trying to recapture lost athletic glory at my age"; "I can't help it, I'm thirty-two going on fifteen").

Then apologize for having taken up her time ("That must have been very tedious for you").

If it's embarrassingly apparent that you were showing off, say in mock solemnity, "I sincerely hope you don't think I was trying to show off." After she snorts, add, "I admit, I'm shameless."

Among the lower orders, such showing off is called courtship display. The peacock spreads his feathers, rams butt heads, and flies follow elaborate mating dances. It works for them. It can work for you.

Hypnosis

Most women, ever eager to be the center of attention, will willingly offer themselves as subjects for hypnosis if you can convince them you're an expert.

Don't expect actually to hypnotize her. Despite tales of people jumping off buildings or committing murder while hypnotized, any realistic study of the field will show that few subjects can be persuaded to place their hands in fire or do anything they wouldn't do normally. Hypnosis is merely the power of suggestion, and people will generally do only what they want. Herein lies the trick.

If the girl wants sex (this includes most of them) but feels that she ought not to have it with you at this particular moment (this also includes most of them), "hypnosis" can provide her with just the excuse she needs.

Thus you must convince your subject not that she is hypnotized but that she can convince you (or herself) that she is hypnotized. To effect this charade, it is not necessary to have her stand on her head while speaking in tongues. Less drama is called for.

Start by repeating over and over in a rhythmic monotone that she feels very relaxed. Instruct her to hold her arms straight out. Then tell her they feel increasingly heavy. (This requires no great leap of imagination.) Next, tell her she feels drowsy. Continue to tell her how relaxed she feels. Suggest that she feels warm, and would be more comfortable with fewer clothes. Tell her that the massage you're giving her is relaxing her even further. With her "free will" supposedly taken away, she'll feel free to do (and let you do) as she pleases.

She may jokingly blame you afterward for having "hypnotized" her into having sex, anxious to deny complicity in the act.

However, the essential judgment to make beforehand is not how hypnotizable she is but rather how much of a liar.

Pretend You're Married

People often complain that in this era of free sex, the forbidden fruit appeal of sex has disappeared. Well, married men are one of the few taboos left. So why not make yourself seem unattainable? It's easy to do. Just pretend you're married. (In these plague-ridden times, it's also an excellent way of advertising you're disease-free.)

The traditional line used by the average husband is that his wife is a shrew, and he'd like to leave her and marry the target instead. This tactic sometimes meets with success, which is why, of course, it has become a tradition.

However, the opposite (and less clichéd) approach will yield more bountiful results. Wax eloquent about how wonderful your wife and marriage are. This will put your target off her guard: No guy on the make talks about how wonderful his wife is. And it poses a subconscious challenge few women can resist. (If she can distract such a happily married man, she must be quite attractive indeed.)

35

If your target needs a little encouragement, test the waters by commenting, "If I wasn't married, you're the first one I'd ask out." If she responds favorably, you're home free.

If you commit a *faux pas*, you've got a built-in excuse: "God, it's been so long since I've actually tried to seduce anybody, this kind of stuff just feels awkward to me now."

The hard-core homebreakers will take it as a challenge to see how long they can keep you from home. Nothing works better than, "Gee, my wife must be getting worried." Once you're at the homebreaker's apartment, make the following bogus call (dial eight digits): "Hello, honey? I'm at the office, I have to work late on the new project . . . a couple of hours . . . love you, bye-bye." She'll do anything to keep you from getting home on time.

Every night, armies of married men slip off their wedding bands, trying to conceal their attached state. They should be flaunting it. And so should you, whether or not you're married.

So invest in a wedding ring. It will never occur to your prospect that you're single. Even better, it will never occur to her to try to wrangle some kind of commitment from you.

If You're Divorced

If your target knows you're divorced, her natural tendency is to be swayed by a latent sense of sisterhood and disbelieve your version of events. To counteract these instincts, you must tread very delicately. You must put the subject in such a light as to enlist her sympathy. There are certain things you can say, and certain things you cannot.

You can't say, "She was always arguing with me," a statement that gives off faint reverberations of, "The bitch didn't know how to take orders."

Don't complain bitterly of your ex's spending habits, or your complaint will echo, "Cheap ... cheap ... cheap."

You mustn't criticize your ex's poor housekeeping, or your target will assume you didn't do any yourself. It also brings to mind the image of domestic slavery—which will not evoke feelings of romance.

Do not say that your ex cheated on you. While this will elicit sympathy, it will also make you look like a pathetic cuckold, and your target will wonder why your ex felt the need to cheat—didn't you satisfy her?

Likewise, don't admit that you were caught cheating—a clear indication that you will also cheat on your target.

You cannot even remotely imply, "She got old and I got tired of her."

If your ex has a restraining order on you, don't breathe a word of that.

Here is what you can say:

If you have children, note that she ignored them and didn't take care of them. This implies no fault on your part and makes your ex look quite coldhearted.

Or say your ex was chemically dependent. Don't explode in righteous anger at the recollection. Just shake your head sadly and calmly say, "There was a problem with alcohol there," or "When we got married, I didn't fully appreciate that . . . that she used drugs." This shows tremendous forbearance.

Mournfully mumble, "No matter how many times I tried to get professional help for her, she'd always backslide. I just couldn't bear to watch her do that to herself." Only a saint could put up with an addict for an extended time, and if you fall short of sainthood, well, that's forgivable.

The nerviest approach of all, if you can get away with it, is to claim that you've been married and divorced five times. Everyone has heard of people like this, but very few people have actually met one. While your target won't regard you as a good prospect for a long-term marriage, she'll be fascinated the way a bird is mesmerized by a snake.

Play your cards right and you may just be dealing with the future ex Mrs. you.

Be a Widower

If you are thirty-five and still unmarried, the only conclusion a girl can draw is that you're not interested in marriage—and this will diminish her interest in you. If you are divorced, your target will wonder why your marriage failed. (Are you a philanderer? A wife-beater? Or just plain selfish?)

The solution is to pose as a widower. Evidence of your Dear Departed needn't be overwhelming, just a framed picture or two on the bedstand. (Your prospect would prefer less rather than more evidence of the deceased.)

Your wife died of leukemia almost two years ago (an exact date lends credibility). Anything longer than two years and you might have turned into a hound again; anything less and she'd wonder why you don't seem sad. Leukemia conjures up the image of you faithfully standing vigil at her bedside during those last agonizing months. (Being able to summon tears at will is a tremendous advantage.)

If she blurts out, "That must have been terrible when she died," simply reply, "Any words to describe it would sound trite. Reminisce ("We used to walk here all the time") but stop short of "I'll never love another the way I loved her." It enhances your marriageability to muse, "Right before she got sick, we had just decided to have kids." Always conclude,

"Well—I guess I can't spend the rest of my life mourning her."

It won't occur to your prospect that you are lying unless you get carried away and contradict yourself. As always, the minimalist school of lying works best.

Sympathy Booty

All women harbor the maternal instinct. Although usually suppressed, it's not buried deeply; the slightest provocation can bring it to the surface. How do you focus it on yourself?

Simply relate a story that makes you look tragic but not pathetic, sad but not creepy.

"Last week the doctor told me that I only have half a year to live because of my brain tumor." The Florence Nightingale in any woman will compel her to do anything in her power to ease the pain of your last months. (The only drawback here is you can't continue to enjoy her after the six months are over.)

"When I was ten I was molested by an older man." This makes you look like a sexual victim rather than the victimizer you are.

"Ever since my wife died of cancer last year I haven't been able to feel much of anything for another woman." No woman can resist this challenge. (Tony Curtis used it to good effect with Marilyn Monroe in *Some Like It Hot*.)

Be brave. Always insist, no matter how heartrending your problem, that you don't want sympathy.

Pretend It's Your Birthday

When a woman knows it's your birthday, it seems to strike a generous chord somewhere deep inside. If you let her know subtly, she may even feel slightly guilty she hasn't gotten you a present. It will also give the two of you an excuse to "celebrate" (for most people any excuse will do).

At an opportune moment, ask, "Do I get a birthday kiss?" She will be hard put to say no. After all, it would take a very hard-hearted (or very suspicious) woman to refuse a *birthday* kiss. A birthday kiss sounds chaste, but physically it's the same as any other: upper persuasion for a lower invasion.

If this doesn't lead to immediate results, ask for a massage. Or jokingly suggest that what you'd really like for your birthday is to see her in her birthday suit.

Unless she knows you well, chances are she won't ask you for proof that it's your birthday.

Can You Keep a Secret?

If you know a woman on a flirtatious but not intimate basis, and see her regularly—for instance, in between classes or every morning at a coffee shop—ask if she can keep a secret.

When she says yes, look around to make sure no one else is within earshot, and whisper conspiratorially, "You've got an incredibly beautiful face."

If you get a positive reaction to this, next time you see her, tell her she's got great legs.

Next time, tell her those great legs lead up to a scrumptious rumptious.

Next time, say she's got beautiful breasts.

Each time, start by asking if she can keep a secret. She will, of course, say yes, since nobody admits they can't keep a secret. Then, when you tell her the "secret," she will have tacitly agreed to be part of your little cabal.

Judge from her reaction each time whether she'll be receptive to escalating levels of boldness. If she reacts laughingly, take the next step. If not, simply stop, having offended her only slightly. (How offended can she be by a compliment?)

Next, ask her if she can keep a secret, then tell her you'd like to lay some kisses on her legs. Next, her rump. Next, her breasts. Finally, ask her if there's a time you could plant these kisses on her. Any woman with even a vestigial sense of modesty will feel obliged to say no, so ask if you could just buy her dinner instead. If she has let the flirting get to this stage, she will probably accept.

With a little luck on your part, after the date she'll be hoping you're the one who can keep a secret.

Playing the Ethnic Angle

There are three ways to exploit your target's ethnicity: flattery, teasing, or claiming consanguinity. The choice depends on your target.

Some women (and some ethnic groups) have to be treated with kid gloves. These you should flatter. Flattery generally consists of praising the accomplishments (or sympathizing with the travails) of her group. Another common approach is to claim as your hero a kinsman of hers. Unfortunately, such attempts at flattery are often painfully transparent, and leave both of you feeling awkward.

Tell her she looks like whatever you are. If she's smart, she realizes people often like to claim a good-looking person as one of their own. This is an unintended and therefore more sincere form of flattery.

Another approach is to tease her. When she first tells you what her antecedents are, ask, "Are you ashamed of that?" Later, comment, "You're very well behaved for an Italian."

Or try, "Back in the old country, wasn't there a lot of inbreeding among your people? Don't anthropologists explain your country's history that way?"

Whatever you do, make sure your jibes are gentle ones

that could be aimed at any group (such as Polish jokes). Well-aimed barbs at your own group, however, are acceptable.

If it's at all possible, claim consanguinity. Tell her you're part whatever she is. (Kinship begets trust, and trust begets intimacy.) If you can convince her that you share her ethnicity (to whatever small extent), be sure to mention how much happier her mother would be if she knew that her daughter had a nice Italian boyfriend.

If you can't convince her that you're of the same ethnicity, at least make a joke of it. Say, "You don't think those are my real parents, do you? I was adopted from a Lithuanian adoption agency." Or try, "The [your group] are lost descendants of the [her group]. Recent archaeological finds have confirmed this."

Find out which little town her great-grandparents came from, then say that your great-grandparents came from there, too. And come to think of it, you had Scepettos in your family line. Nothing lends that feeling of immediate closeness like knowing you're cousins three times removed. (It will also lend the extra spice of incest to the relationship.)

Posing as a Foreigner

Ever notice how when you're in a foreign country you can just throw yourself at people's mercy and they're usually very helpful? There's no reason not to do the same thing at home. Just ask a pretty woman in ungrammatical, halting English if she can direct you to a good restaurant. (When she answers, pretend you don't understand, the better to draw out the conversation.)

When she asks what country you're from, be believable (i.e., if you're blond, don't say Tanzania). Whatever you look like don't say France, because everyone who has taken a little high school French will want to try it out on you. (On that score, rest assured no one knows Bulgarian, Cantonese, or Ibo.) If you're not good with accents, just say you're Canadian. After you've managed to get the directions to a good restaurant, ask her if she'll be your guest. Relay—awkwardly—that you'd be very grateful if you could practice your English with her.

As a foreigner you can get away with all sorts of gaucheries that would be unforgivable were you an American. In fact, she'll probably think they're cute. For instance, while you're talking about your country, point at your chest; then, when talking about her country, point at her chest, lightly touching her breast with your finger.

The most satisfying aspect of this encounter comes after you've had sex, seeing her expression when you announce in your normal voice, "Well, honey, that's your lesson in foreign culture for today."

Your Hero

If your target places a premium on virtue, you can leave the impression that you share the same values by talking about someone you admire. That someone cannot be one of your actual heroes—a macho football player, a playboy actor, or an influential billionaire. You must pretend to admire a saint.

Bring up the subject by asking your target who her heroes are, as if you want to know her better. Feign fascination with her reply. Then, if your target fails to ask you the same question, prompt her with, "I always find it interesting who people's heroes are." She should pick up on this cue. If she doesn't, plow ahead anyway: "You know, I've always admired . . ."

Candidates for your pantheon include Mother Teresa, Albert Schweitzer, and Father Damien. Shrug resignedly: "I wish I were that good. But I'm afraid I'm a sinner." (Everyone knows sinners are more fun.)

If your candidate has a little bit of the gold-digger to her (most women harbor a latent tendency), add, "I'm too interested in things like money. Well, maybe someday." She'll find it reassuring that you intend to get rich first. No woman minds being with a rich saint.

Another tactic is to rave about what a gentleman a certain friend is. Spin a yarn about how your friend had said his girlfriend broke up with him when in fact he broke up with her and you only discovered the truth accidentally when you talked to her later on. ("I figure most guys are doing well enough by not exaggerating their exploits. I never figured I'd meet a guy who'd lie the other way. What a *great guy*!") The implication is that you might be inspired to behave similarly. (Don't use a buddy she knows or she won't believe you.)

Impress her with your virtuousness and you may get to impress her with your virtuosity later on.

Paying For It

You're at your wits' end. You've tried every trick you know to get your date into bed, but she is behaving like an immovable object, forcing you to the unpleasant conclusion that you're not an irresistible force.

There's one last hope: Her greed may outweigh her pride.

Look her straight in the eye and say, "I'd give anything to make love to you." Pull out your wallet and whisper, "Even two hundred dollars." Lay the bills down—but overact just a touch, to leave open the possibility that you're kidding.

If two hundred dollars doesn't do the trick, and you can afford it, offer more. You can always take the money back right after you finish; there's very little she can do about that. Or just tell her you'll pay her the next day, then don't. It's hardly the type of thing she'd take you to court for.

Don't make the mistake of thinking she's not "that type of woman," because every woman has her price.

If She Likes Her Men Macho

While the book thus far has concentrated on how to show you're sensitive and caring, there are women who want a Stanley Kowalski.

The secret to appearing tough is never to appear to try to seem tough. A good tactic is to talk about how scared you were in some dangerous situation most people would never dream of getting into. ("The first time I went skydiving I almost pissed in my pants. Couldn't wait to get up the second time, though.")

If she asks where you went to school, tell her Bridgewater Prep. When she says she hasn't heard of it, grin and comment, "I don't imagine too many of your friends went to reform school."

A tattoo will further burnish the image. (Just get the kind you stick on and wash off.) The skull and crossed rifles motif lends just the right touch.

Casually mention your stretch in Folsom. ("I was a frightened boy when I went in, I was an animal when I got out.") If she asks what you were in for, answer, "armed robbery" ("I was young and I was foolish").

If the subject turns to sports, yours used to be kick-boxing. ("Not that noncontact bullshit.") No matter how small you are, there's a weight class for you.

Other facts to remember: You grew up poor; you understand cars inside and out but know nothing you'd learn from a book; and your politics are three steps to the right of Attila the Hun.

Always use ethnic slurs. And remember that your testosterone level is suspect if you pay any attention to traffic lights.

This type of woman likes a man who's assertive, so don't act tentative when you move in for the clinch.

Save Her Life

How many adventure movies don't have at least one scene where the hero saves the beauty's life? In how many of those adventures does the woman not fall for the hero? Tells you something, doesn't it?

Even if the woman doesn't fall for you, if you save a woman's life it would be incredibly petty of her not to give up the booty.

If you're not in a position to save your target's life, simply set up such a situation. If you have a buddy she hasn't met before (preferably a threatening-looking fellow), arrange with him to meet up with you and your date in a relatively secluded area. Make sure he has a weapon (a starter's pistol will do, but be sure it's unloaded), and apply your talents as a choreographer. The scene should run roughly as follows:

You and your date are walking down a lonely country road, and your buddy rushes up, pulls out his gun, and says, "Hand over your money and I won't hurt you." You kick the gun out of his hand (tell him beforehand to hold it low), then place your foot on his stomach and send him sprawling. You scramble over to retrieve the gun, and the "mugger" runs away.

Take a deep breath, look as if you're trying to hold back your anger, and say, "One of these days I'm going to meet someone like that and hurt him . . . bad."

Then wink at your target and yell at the retreating figure, "Hey, you forgot your gun!"

She's yours.

The most enjoyable part of this escapade will come after you've tagged her, and after you've grown tired of her, when you introduce her to your buddy.

Relaxing a Nervous Woman

If a woman is nervous, it's not just her problem. It's also *your* problem, because a nervous woman doesn't feel sexy.

The solution is to make her feel she's not alone in her nervousness. Nothing makes a nervous Nellie less nervous than the knowledge that you, too, are nervous. So even if you're so relaxed you're on the verge of falling asleep, tell her that you were racked with anxiety before asking her out, you were a nervous wreck before meeting her, and you're a basket case right now.

Or just say, "You intimidate me." If she expresses surprise, mention that you're not used to being around someone so accomplished. Then list her accomplishments (there's got to be *something* she's good at). Knowing that you're intimidated will relax her, and also give her that warm glow that comes from being appreciated.

Sometimes during a first date the tension builds until the

pass is made, because both parties know it is coming; use that as an excuse to kiss her early. Just say, "Forgive me, but I think this will make both of us a little less nervous," and kiss her. Then say, "Now you don't have to worry about me making a pass at you anymore."

You can also take some of the pressure off her by saying, "Listen, I'm not ready to sleep with you tonight, so let's just talk. Okay?" She may resent the implicit assumption that *she's* ready to sleep with *you*, but in a subtle way it will make her feel a little less like the meat in the lion's cage.

Tease Her About Her Age

As the sociologists constantly remind us, ours is a culture that worships youth. If you are chasing a woman several years your senior, she will undoubtedly be painfully aware of that difference. Teasing her about it will bring an awkward subject out into the open and make her more relaxed about it.

So if she's six years older than you, tell her she's old enough to be your mother.

Or tell her she looks like an older version of so-and-so.

Tell her she reminds you of a woman whose only public image is that of an older woman, such as Golda Meir, Margaret Thatcher, or Indira Gandhi. If she tells you about some altruistic act of hers, tell her she's just like Mother Teresa. When she protests that she is not nearly that good, say that oh, no, you meant the way she looks.

Ask to see a picture of her when she was young.

Ask if she's embarrassed to be robbing the cradle.

Ask her impression of the decade she was born in, as if she would have been old enough to have formed a distinct impression of the era's popular culture when in fact she was only a toddler. (If she was born in the midsixties, ask if she went to Woodstock, and so on.)

Benjamin Franklin once said that older women are superior because they are grateful for the attention they receive. This may be true, but they are generally not grateful when that attention is directed at their age, unless it is done in a lighthearted, teasing sort of way calculated to put them at ease about what they might otherwise consider a deep, dark secret.

Wistfulness

For many women, sentiment is an unavoidable stepping-stone to horniness. Here are a few standard clichés designed to put things in the right perspective for them.

If your target is approaching thirty, touch on the subject indirectly. "They say youth is wasted on the young. It's so true." Or, "So many people don't take advantage of their youth and beauty, then regret it later on."

The brevity-of-life theme strikes a responsive chord in most women. "When you think in terms of evolutionary time, we're not even here for the blink of an eyelash. Life is so ephemeral, it's a shame not just to reach out and enjoy every day as much as you possibly can."

If your target is holding out on you, continue in this vein. "When you're seventy years old and your life is behind you, do you think you'll be happy you were virtuous and chaste, or do you think you just might regret your missed opportunities?" Or say, "Look around. See all these people? In ninety years every one of them, including you and me, will be long dead and buried. Then it will be too late."

Put it in historical perspective. "Catherine of Russia used to enjoy a different man every night. The Empress Wu of China had a bed constructed so she could enjoy thirty-three men at the same time. All I'm asking you to do is enjoy one man, the same man, for a long time." If the discussion drags on, ask, "Would you rather live your life or just talk about it?"

Tell her, "I used to be like you. I always used to live for tomorrow. One day I woke up and realized I had to live for today."

If you can stomach all these clichés, they should put your target in a more pliant frame of mind. If you're with a woman you find barely attractive, these lines are a good way to convince yourself to go for it.

Paying Lip Service to Friendship

One of the great myths is that a man and a woman can be just friends, with no sex involved. This myth, popular among women, implies that men enjoy their company, prize their conversation, and value their friendship. In reality, almost no heterosexual men hang out with heterosexual women on a regular basis with absolutely no sex (or attempts at sex) involved.

However, to pass the Nice Guy Litmus Test, you must prove you're capable of being a "friend" in a low-key, no-strings-attached sort of way. This allows your target to feel that the two of you have a solid basis for a long-term relationship, and also allows her to feel less pressured for sex.

Mention early on in the courtship process, "Oh, I have lots of friends who are women. You know, just friends." This will show you to be the sincere, warmhearted individual you aren't.

The irony is that once you are involved in a sexual relationship (often only after having arduously proven capable of a nonsexual one), friendships with other women are not countenanced. Just try telling your new steady girlfriend that you're going out to have a drink with another woman—you know, just as friends.

Female logic has never been known for its logic.

Pretend to Be Someone Else

You've just phoned your target and arranged a date, but the conversation was flat and stilted. If you want to inject some levity into your budding relationship, phone her back and pretend to be your own parole officer. (Make sure she knows you well enough to know you're kidding.)

Say that you've put a tracer on Nick's line and just wanted to check up and make sure that Nick was behaving himself. Ask if she thinks Nick should be put back in jail, and if Nick has been causing any trouble. Your target, if she has a sense of humor, will seize this opportunity to make all sorts of outrageous charges against you. Play along.

When she asks what Nick was in jail for, say sex crimes. When she asks what sort of sex crimes, tell her that several women lodged charges that Nick was too good in bed, that he ruined them for other men. When your target says that she didn't know that was a crime, answer that in your county it is. Say that Nick has learned his lesson, and he has agreed never to be that good in bed again.

Or you can pretend to be Nick's psychiatrist. When she asks why Nick's seeing a psychiatrist, reply that Nick had a nervous breakdown because of a woman he was dating who insulted him. List the warning signs of an impending break-down (things you've already done), and stress that she should be extremely nice to Nick and accede to all Nick's demands. She'll probably say that she's not sure she can do that, as

Nick has been making quite a few demands. Stress that any resistance on her part would be a traumatic enough blow to cause a relapse. The next time you see her, pretend ignorance of the conversation and play off it.

This kind of repartee will not necessarily land your target in bed, but at least it will put the two of you on a joking, relaxed footing—a better vantage point from which to get her there.

If you do end up in bed, and after a few weeks it gets a bit boring, close your eyes and pretend that *she's* someone else.

A Solitary Sport

Unlike real wolves, the human kind does better not to hunt in packs. Despite the occasional situation where a buddy comes in handy, as a rule you'll enjoy more success if you search for prey alone.

Guys in groups tend to approach girls only to show off to each other (this is especially true during high school). In fact, most guys who make ostensible pickup attempts in front of their gang would have no idea how to respond if a woman actually reacted favorably to their advances. (Women sense this, and this is part of the reason why comments from such groups tend to make them angry.)

No woman can do other than ignore a group of guys making lewd comments. Even if the guys were friendly in a polite way, she would feel vaguely that she was inviting a gang bang by being friendly. (And if she didn't feel this way, she still might be confused about which guy she was supposed to respond to.)

And even if she wasn't confused, it would still be hard to let one of them pick her up in front of all the others; after all, it's harder to do anything with an audience. (Think of it as the difference between having sex in private and onstage.)

So see the guys when you want to see the guys, not when you want to meet women. Besides, as with other carnivores who hunt in packs, there is always the conflict in the end about who gets the meat.

Part II
Props

Score with Your Football

When a woman sees you tossing a football, she immediately perceives you as nonthreatening. If you're over twenty-five years old, yelling "And Namath is fading back! Namath is fading back!" as you throw the ball will make you appear particularly innocent. After all, can you imagine Charlie Manson playing football? Neither can she.

Women normally don't frequent football fields (if they do, you needn't bother with props), so you'll want to take your football into town. Have your buddy pass you the ball near a pretty woman, then when it goes bouncing in some crazy direction (preferably hers), apologize for bothering her. If you're lucky, the football will hit her, allowing you to tender heartfelt apologies and perhaps start a conversation.

But this also can backfire. It's more productive simply to ask the woman if she'd like to join your game. If she claims she doesn't know how to play, reply, "You're probably better than Joey over there." (Boyish banter will augment your air of innocence.) If she says she's not dressed properly, look puzzled and reply, "This is touch, not tackle." If she still declines, which she undoubtedly will, say, "Catch!" and gently toss her the ball. Her instinct will be to hold out her arms, and, before she knows it, she's involved. If she says she has to go somewhere—for instance the opera—reply, "Come on, what's more fun, the opera or a football game? Get serious!"

The best thing about the football pass is that you leave no tracks. If you try to hit on every prospect at a party, eventually no self-respecting woman there will have anything to do with you. If you fail to score with your football, just take it around the corner, start your routine anew, and no one's the wiser.

The Business Card

If you have a respectable job at a respectable company, use your business card to advantage.

You're on the train to work. You've been staring at the woman across the way and even made eye contact a couple of times, but haven't thought of an appropriate opening line. Just before your stop, dart over with an apologetic look on your face. "Listen, it's awfully forward of me to say this to a complete stranger, but I couldn't help but notice how beautiful you are. I know it's obnoxious to hand out a business card, but here," you say, handing her your card. "Give me a call tomorrow, please."

You mustn't seem as if this is a habit. And you can't seem pleased with yourself (or your job) as you do it, otherwise she'll be turned off by your conceit. You must come across flustered when you do this, as if you were goaded into this act of desperation by her beauty.

When a woman calls, don't ask, "Which one were you?" Just say, "Oh, I was hoping you would call" and see if you can tell from the conversation which one she was.

If you have a fancy job, you may attract gold-diggers with this approach. If you do, so what? You're not looking to marry them.

It pays to keep some monkey business cards on hand.

Your Bodyguard

If you have a buddy who's large or tough-looking, preferably both, you can impress the impressionable by pretending he's your bodyguard. This game works best with gold-diggers and starfuckers, but even normal women will be bamboozled by the aura of a fellow who needs a bodyguard.

Your buddy should dress in a suit and tie (only lowlifes have bodyguards who don't dress formally) and double as your chauffeur. Rent a limousine for the evening (it's cheaper than you think without the driver).

Your buddy drives, you sit in the back, and you stop whenever you see a pretty woman. He gets out, walks up to the woman, takes off his chauffeur's cap, and politely says, "Excuse me, miss, but Mr. Casanova saw you and would like to meet you." He then gestures toward the rear of the car. Press the button to roll the window down and when the woman leans over to see who's in the backseat, simply say, "You're a very pretty woman. Can I offer you a ride?"

If she accepts, act blasé, as if you are merely accepting your due. You must be very low key and not appear eager. Whatever you do, don't smirk or give yourself away with any stifled laughs.

Be sure to refer to your buddy as your bodyguard, so she gets the message. If your target asks why you need a bodyguard, just reply vaguely, "Lot of bad people out there." When you get out of the car, he should follow you at a discreet distance.

When she asks what you do for a living, pick a role that suits you (e.g., if you're nerdy-looking, don't claim to be a rock star). If you're barely out of college, you probably should just invent a role for your father.

To make it worthwhile for your buddy, just switch roles occasionally. (It's almost as much fun to play the tough bodyguard anyway.)

You're not going to start any long-term relationships this way, but who wants one when numerous short-term relationships are available?

Pull it off, and you may well need a bodyguard just to protect you from all the angry women you've lied to.

A Little Pooch Can Lead to a Little Chooch

The dog is truly man's best friend.

The only thing that makes a woman glow more than praising her dog is praising her child, and the advantage of the former is that chances are it's not her offspring.

So if you see an attractive woman walking her dog, stroll right up and pet it. Don't worry about scaring her. A guy who likes dogs seems sexless and nonthreatening. Face it: A guy who lets his dog eat off his plate simply couldn't be a womanizer. And she'll be pleased that somebody finally appreciates how lovable her dog is.

So pat its head, scratch behind its ears, talk baby talk to it, and let it sniff your crotch. Be rough, like a real dog owner. If you can bear it, kneel down and let it lick your face—the ultimate proof you like dogs. Repulsive as this is, you may be setting in motion a chain of events that will culminate in your licking its owner.

Meanwhile, don't even glance at the woman. Tell her how cute her dog is, ask what breed it is, and reminisce about old Fido—who just happened to be the spitting image of her dog—and how you cried when he was killed by a car.

Be subtle as you steer the conversation from her dog to her. ("Isn't it hard keeping a dog around here? Do you live nearby? As a matter of fact, I'm thinking about getting a one-bedroom there myself. I should check one out sometime. Gee, that would be awfully nice of you.")

If the woman rejects your overtures, a good way to work out your anger (it's unhealthy to bottle it up) is to spit on the dog as you walk away.

Your Dog

Having your own dog can be a great conversation starter. Many people have owned dogs at some time, and feel a bond with other owners. Often dogs can bring back pleasant memories of childhood.

Don't buy an intimidating beast. Many men feel the need

65

for a dog that enhances their sense of masculinity. But Dobermans, Rottweilers, and pit bulls are not cuddly and do not attract friendly female attention.

On the other hand, you don't want a neurotic little poodle or Chihuahua, which send the opposite message. Labs and golden retrievers strike a nice balance.

A woman who would never dream of approaching you if you were alone will think nothing of coming up to ask about your dog. And unloading her maternal instincts on your pet puts her in a relaxed, receptive frame of mind.

Train your dog to go to women, wag its tail and sniff, but not to bark ferociously. This will give you the opportunity to say, "Sorry to bother you. He seems to like you," and start a conversation.

It is a truism that a man who treats his dog well will treat his wife well. Even if a woman hasn't heard this, she will instinctively sense it. So no matter what kind of husband you intend to be, while courting, lavish affection on your pet.

Having a dog is almost a public declaration that you have affection to spare: not a bad subterfuge for a fellow with lust to spare.

If you don't want the hassle of actually owning a dog, offer to walk a friend's. Just be sure to get acquainted with the animal beforehand. It wouldn't do to have the animal attack you just as you're trying to ingratiate yourself with some dog-loving woman.

Your Lair

Whether you live in a dormitory, a rented apartment, or your own house, certain universal rules of decorating apply.

First, be clean. You may not mind accumulating a leaning tower of pizza boxes, and you may think taking out the garbage a waste of time, but assume your target feels differently. She won't want to lie down amid the trash (no matter how well you feel she'd blend in).

If you have roommates, make sure they're out of eyeshot and earshot.

Decoration designed to augment your masculinity will make you seem either very young or very insecure. Off-color signs ("Lie down. I'm a psychiatrist" or "Trespassers will be violated") will make you appear particularly juvenile.

Pictures of past girlfriends or anything remotely resembling a trophy collection are to be kept out of sight. (A pair of panties nailed to the wall guarantees you won't get hers off.)

A bedroom with a large water bed and a mirror on the ceiling will make her uneasy. And sexual paraphernalia are most definitely to be kept out of sight.

Absolutely do not post centerfolds from girlie magazines. No woman will disrobe in their presence. She won't want the comparison. (Not to mention that you'll come across the type who spends more time masturbating than making love.) Put yourself in her shoes. Imagine she had three photographs of erect penises on her wall, labeled "9"," "10"," and "11"." Would you find this conducive to a romantic evening?

Mood Music

Ever noticed how the background music plays such a large part in setting the mood for a movie? Horror scenes are more terrifying, action scenes more exciting, and romantic scenes more moving. And most of the time, you don't even notice the music; it merely works insidiously on your subconscious.

Well, music works its magic on women, too. You can take advantage of this if she's at your place.

Euphoria-inducing dance music, especially of the Motown variety, is a good way to start the evening on an upbeat note. Then, as attack time draws near, sentimental music will put her in the mood. Serenade her with Tchaikovsky (his three ballets), "Moon River," or any show tune (from a show with a sappy ending).

Don't play your music too loudly. The trick is to alter her mood subtly, not blast her out of her senses. Background music must remain there.

Match your music to your target. If she considers herself a feminist, don't play Elvis. If she considers herself sophisticated, don't play country and western.

No matter what she considers herself, don't play John Philip Sousa or Gregorian chants. Just play soft music with an insistent beat.

Music is the food of love. Make sure she eats hearty.

Home Movies

One underrated technique for putting a woman in the mood is a pornographic film. This does not mean taking your date to the local X-rated theater, an experience as sordid as it is potentially embarrassing. Instead, keep a porn film near your VCR. The choice of hard- or soft-core should depend on your audience.

Don't display the tape front and center stage, but do put it where she won't fail to notice it. Have only one porn video in view: a single tape suggests open-mindedness, a library, perversion.

Don't propose a viewing yourself; let her suggest it, as her curiosity should get the better of her. If she just points at it and laughs smarmily, which is probably what she'll do, ask if she'd like to see it. If she makes a derogatory comment, tell her she should watch it before passing judgment.

Any shame she feels about wanting to see the film should be overcome by your greater implicit shame for having actually purchased it. (Tell her you got it before you had some buddies over one evening.) During the movie, express boredom so she doesn't feel threatened by the presence of a sexually aroused, dangerous male.

Don't assume she'll become overtly aroused by the film (although this may happen). She may even feel disgust. But the viewing should plant a seed in her mind that won't disappear until it has sprouted and grown ripe for the plucking.

Part III
Situations

The Challenge

As January 1 approaches, people think of New Year's resolutions: getting to the gym three times a week, forgoing desserts, and visiting Aunt Mary more often. It's time for you to challenge a buddy to a scoring contest: Get out the old tote board and see who can print with the most women in the following calendar year.

Choose a buddy who will tell the truth, the whole truth, and nothing but the truth about his exploits; otherwise it becomes a lying contest. He should be roughly as prolific as you. Otherwise the competition will be a humiliation for one and a bore for the other.

It is remarkable what a boosting effect such a contest can have on your numbers. When you're neck and neck in an exciting race, your every sense will keenly attune to the hunt. Your mind will focus, your wits sharpen, and your carnivorous instincts erupt in all their glory. You should have your best year ever.

If you find yourself lowering your standards to an embarrassing extent in the scramble for points, you can always tell yourself, "Ah, I just did that one because of the contest."

This book is devoted to changing your target's mind-set. Changing your own can have an even more salutory effect on your dance card.

At the Gym

Twenty years ago, most women thought if they so much as touched a barbell, they would wake up the next morning looking like Mr. Universe. Today the average woman goes to her gym five times as often as she goes to her hairdresser.

In recent years, health clubs have acquired a reputation as the new singles bars. In fact, they're better. The healthy, athletic atmosphere is more conducive to other physical activities (and leotards hide few secrets from an undecided suitor).

One way to meet a prospective target is to see what kind of gym bag she has, get the same kind, take hers, "find out" whose bag you took "by accident," and offer to buy her a drink by way of apology. But there are easier ways.

If you don't mind appearing a novice, ask, "How do you use this machine?" Likewise, asking a woman for help with negatives (continuing past the point where you can lift the weight entirely by yourself) is a good icebreaker.

If you're looking to start a conversation with a woman on the treadmill next to yours, ask, "Do you ever feel, as I do, that this machine is a metaphor for your life?"

Try flattery. "You must have very low body fat" is acceptable in this milieu; or, "You must work on your quadriceps a lot." (Most women don't even know what quadriceps are and will ask.) "Nice pecs" might get a rise (the pectoral muscles are those of the chest).

"Are you a dancer?" is effective because no woman minds being mistaken for a dancer. (Don't ask if she's a shot-putter. And "Are you on steroids?," while flattering to a guy, will not have the same effect on a woman.)

Ask, "Why is it women never sweat?" If she is only lifting a tiny amount of weight, ask, "How did you get so strong?" (Be sure your humor is obviously good-natured.)

Bet her an ice cream cone that you can lift twice as much weight at a certain station. Whoever wins, you've got a date. (If you're riding the stationary bike next to hers, challenge her to a race.)

If you don't score, at least you won't have to gnash your teeth over a wasted evening (there are times a good workout is more satisfying anyway).

At the Beach

You're at the beach, the hot summer sun giving your libido a boost. Young women lie around in various states of undress, some with the upper parts of their bikinis tantalizingly undone. And the only thing you can do about it is jump into the cold water.

How do you approach a bikini without being overly intrusive?

Bring a six-pack in a Styrofoam container. Walk up to a woman with a towel draped over your arm like a waiter and ask, "Would you care for a cocktail before dinner?" If she plays along and asks for a martini, reply, "I'm sorry but we're out of those. We *do* have beer, however."

Ask her to watch your belongings while you take a dip. After your swim, ask her to put suntan lotion on your back. If you're with friends, ask a group of women if they'd like to participate in your "Beach Olympics." Run a race (you in knee-deep versus them in ankle-deep water); play football with a beach ball; have a swimming race to the buoy and back. Have chicken fights (you and your buddy each carry a woman on your shoulders in chest-deep water and they try to topple one another). Something about wrapping her legs around your neck makes a woman feel intimate with you.

The nice thing about meeting a woman at the beach is that what you see is what you get. No dim light and fancy clothes to disguise the fact that she's twice the woman you thought.

The Wedding

Weddings are festive affairs, with flowers, decorations, ceremony, fancy clothes, new hairdos, and solemn vows of everlasting devotion—all things that women love and men hate. But as long as you're not the one getting married, they are a great trawling spot.

Weddings lend a sort of legitimacy to all the attendees. When you saunter up to a woman on the street, a fear lurks in the back of her mind that you might be a rapist or a serial killer. If you approach a woman at a wedding, this fear does not enter the equation.

Being at a wedding is almost like being set up on a blind

date—you have not only been vouched for as an upstanding member of society, you also have the recommendation of having been liked enough to be invited. So going to a wedding is like being set up on twenty blind dates, but with the blindness eliminated: You get to see which ones are pretty.

You have a natural topic of conversation with any woman there ("How long have you known the bride/groom?, "Isn't it wonderful that they're getting married?")

Single women think of weddings as good hunting grounds themselves, although what many of them are hunting for is a ring. They assume that a single guy who knows a groom is probably looking for a wife himself. Do nothing to disabuse them of that notion.

When a woman gets all gussied up for a ceremony where a man and a woman swear eternal devotion and then she drinks a lot of champagne, it's hard for her not to get into a romantic mood. Take advantage of this vulnerability.

Weddings are great as long as you're not the one being sacrificed on the altar.

Let's Have a Drink

The idea here is not to get drunk unless she does. For while plenty of drunken guys have scored with drunken women, and sober guys with sober women, and sober guys with drunken women, very few drunken guys have scored with sober women.

Restrain yourself to a maximum of two drinks to her one.

If you're not a drinker, do no more than keep pace with her, or rather, get her to keep pace with you.

Propose a toast to her career. If she's not enthusiastic about her work, propose a toast to her early retirement. Or to her favorite hobby. Or to her favorite movie star. Keep proposing personalized toasts, and she will keep drinking. She may even feel obligated to propose some to you after a while. If she does, warn her that you can't be responsible for your actions if she keeps you drinking.

If she's health-conscious, refer to the pseudobeneficial aspects of drinking. ("Studies have shown that people who have a drink a day live longer than teetotalers. Here's to a long life!") Remind her of the B vitamins and brewer's yeast in beer. Refer to the calcium in a Kahlúa and milk. Mention the vitamin C in a vodka and orange juice. If she scoffs at this routine, give up graciously. ("You're right. Oh, well. Kill a few brain cells?")

If she's the type to rise to a dare, challenge her: "I haven't met the woman yet who could chug one of these things." (Make her feminism work in your favor.)

Or say, "Here's a drink that will put some hair on your chest." She'll probably reply she doesn't want any, thank you. You can either reply that you don't believe she doesn't have any, or that she would look good with some. After a few drinks this line of talk will seem amusing.

Try, "One of these and all your troubles will go away," an offer that if true would be hard to resist.

Should the liquor cause you to behave awkwardly, note, "I find that when I've had enough to drink I become incredibly charming. I do all sorts of clever things . . . like throw up."

"Let's have a drink" is the socially acceptable way of saying, "Let's have sex." If a woman accepts the former invitation it is no guarantee that she will accept the latter, but it certainly increases the odds.

At the Supermarket

Some women go to bars, some go to the beach, and some go to the nightclubs. But all women go to buy food. So whatever kind of woman you're in the mood for, you can do all your shopping at the supermarket.

Your opening gambit should depend on what she has in her cart (or on the checkout counter). Ask, "How do you cook that?" or "What do you use those for?" Most women are only too pleased to show their expertise as cooks and potential homemakers.

Or try being playful. If she has two soft drinks and a package of corn chips, try, "That looks like a nutritious meal" or "Health food nut, eh?"

If her shopping cart is absolutely loaded, try, "Like to eat, eh?" or "Need some help eating all of that?" If she's thin, say, "You must have the metabolism of a hummingbird." Flattery never hurts.

If she has a lot of one item, express mock dismay: "Didn't anyone ever teach you about a balanced diet?"

If ice cream is among her purchases, ask, "Whatsamatter . . . no willpower?"

If she has only a couple items, comment, "On a diet, eh?" (Don't try this with a plump woman.)

If she has some particularly vile-looking food, say, "Gee, that looks appetizing" or "You know, you are what you eat."

There are usually an array of sensational tabloids at the

checkout counter. Point out a headline and warn her, "Better watch out: A three-thousand-pound space monster is headed for Earth!" If the headline is gossipy, use that: "Wow! (Such-and-such-a movie star) is two-timing his wife! Can you believe it?"

As you pay for your groceries, ask if you can help carry her bags. If she declines, retort, "You don't understand. I don't charge anything." It's then easier for her to agree because it's as if she's just playing along with a joke.

The way to a woman's heart (and loins) is through your stomach.

Hot Pickup Spots

There are certain places, not normally thought of as pickup joints, where it is easy to catch a woman with her guard down.

If a woman is pondering her tape selection in a video store, she's probably available. (If she were seeing the movie with a boyfriend, he'd be there to help select it.) And if she's looking for entertainment, it means she has spare time on her hands. One natural gambit is, "Don't get that movie unless you want to be bored out of your mind." If a discussion of movies ensues, ask her over to your place to watch a movie.

If you see a woman browsing in a bookstore, point out, "That's a great book." This can lead easily into a conversation about its author, genre, et cetera. Your target will probably feel safe talking to you in this milieu: There's something innocent about a book-lover. (Rapists and murderers generally won't settle for the quiet thrill of a well-constructed paragraph.)

Evening classes tend to attract bored, single women. By their nature these courses encourage chattiness. A little persistence can turn social intercourse into the sexual kind.

The airline terminal is another fertile location. Traveling always gives one a heightened sense of adventure and romance. A woman in this state is always more receptive to male advances. If she's traveling by herself, she is all the more vulnerable. So pack a bag, concoct a plausible story about a trip, head for the nearest airport, and check out the incoming gates. It may be a bit out of the way, but you could just end up as some lucky woman's vacation adventure.

The wise fisherman never goes to the same pond where the other fishermen congregate. He goes to his own private spot where he can land as many fish as he desires.

If You Live in a Small Town

If there's a beauty you know only by sight, and you're probably going to run into her again, you can take a leisurely, two-step approach to picking her up. First, walk up to her and say, "Excuse me, I'm not trying to pick you up or anything, but I just wanted to tell you you're one of the most beautiful women I've ever seen."

She'll undoubtedly wonder who you are and why you're denying it when you're obviously making a play for her.

At this point, hold up your hands in protest and repeat, "I swear, I'm not trying to pick you up. I just wanted to tell you that." Then walk away.

When she recovers her wits, it will occur to her how nice you are to bestow such a compliment and not even be trying to pick her up. As she basks in the warm glow of your flattery, she'll wonder if she will run into you again.

The next time you see her, she will surely greet you enthusiastically, secure in the knowledge that you are all innocence and good intentions. She may even try to find out who you are and if you have any mutual acquaintances. (This will give your compliment more validity in her mind.)

Now that you've established you're not the type who tries to pick up women, you can do exactly that. If she's flirtatious, you might even venture, "Remember what I said about not trying to pick you up? I changed my mind."

When a woman is approached by a stranger, her usual instincts are to shy away. With this approach, she doesn't even get the chance to back off—and she has a while to fantasize about you before she does.

The only hitch to this stratagem is that it is contingent upon running into your prospect again. In New York City, you can use this approach for months on end and never run into the same woman twice.

The Street Approach

Most women seem to have had the "Don't talk to strangers" syndrome instilled at an early age by their mothers. Thus many women who would be friendly at a party will barely be civil if approached on the street. Luckily, there are ways to overcome this barrier.

The problem with "Do you have change for a quarter?" or "Do you have the time?" is that they don't lead naturally into a conversation. That's why, "Haven't I seen you somewhere before?" was actually a clever line—it called for the two of you to compare all the places you'd ever been. Unfortunately, through overuse, the line has become self-parody, and even a variation sounds like a bald pickup attempt.

One alternative is utter sincerity: "Excuse me, this is terribly forward, but I'd be kicking myself for the rest of the day if I let you walk away without at least trying to meet you. Take a chance and have a drink with me. If I offend you, just walk out." If she agrees, half the battle is won. Unfortunately, this type of honesty is rarely appreciated.

The other approach is less dramatic but more effective. Stand on a street corner with an open map. When a pretty woman strolls by, ask her directions for a destination that lies in her path—but is at least five blocks away. There's a good chance she'll say, "Oh, I'm going in that direction," in which case you have a chance to walk—and talk—with her for five blocks. Even if she merely tells you where it is, this is an opportunity to walk alongside and strike up a conversation.

A skillful pickup leaves the woman thinking, "What a lucky coincidence I met that nice man."

Be a Photographer

One of the easiest ways of meeting, flattering, and getting to know a woman is to ask to take her picture. You needn't pose as a foreign tourist, just as a fellow American seeing his own country.

If you carry a camera, you are immediately perceived as nonthreatening. Shutterbugs do not rob, stab, or molest. They're harmless innocents who like to keep photographic memories. (Only nice people keep scrapbooks.)

When you spot a pretty woman, pretend to take a picture of a nearby building or landscape. As she strolls by, ask apologetically if she'd mind if you took her picture. ("Gee, it would certainly add to the picture if you were in it.") Ask her to take your picture, too.

If you have a fancy camera, tell your target you're a professional photographer. This will bring out the aspiring model in every good-looking woman.

If the two of you click, offer to send her the photos. She'll have to give you her address. Her desire for the pictures may even compel her to chat with you. (By acting friendly she may even convince herself that she likes you.)

The photographic approach is also convenient if you like to keep snapshots of your conquests.

Film can be expensive, however, so if you don't want to waste the money, just run through your routine with an empty camera.

Picking Up Women from Your Car

When you're driving, you constantly seem to see good-looking women. Unfortunately, meeting them from your car is an awkward proposition at best.

The problem is, you can't unobtrusively pull over to the side of the road to start a conversation with a woman. An automobile means freedom, power, and adventure, but it also means a traffic jam if you stop in the wrong place.

If you do try it, play off the inherent awkwardness: "Hi. My name's Joe. I was just driving home but—God forgive me—when I saw how beautiful you were, I just had to pull over and try to meet you."

Or ask for directions. If there are two women, it's quite natural for them to say, "Oh, we're going that way. We'll show you." You can offer them a ride if they are going in your direction. (This is one of the few instances where being with a buddy is actually better.)

Once they're in your car, don't try to impress them by speeding. They'll be ill at ease already; you will only scare them further by flooring it.

If you see a beauty at a stoplight, gun your engine to get

her attention and joke, "Race you to the next stoplight." Let her win, then at the next light say, "Okay, okay, I owe you a beer. Where do you want it?"

If you've got a fancy car, your chances improve. It's harder to turn down a ride in a Mercedes (no one is totally immune to status), and an expensive car lends an air of respectability.

Some cars are by their very nature threatening. A pickup truck is intimidating in its overt masculinity, a car with darkened windows automatically connotes sin, and no woman in her right mind is going to climb into a van with a picture of a naked woman on the side.

Unfortunately, most women don't hitchhike anymore. (Ted Bundy ruined it for the rest of us.) Females who do hitchhike are likely to be teenage runaways, a group not noted for personal hygiene. And if you live in a big city, beware of women who favor heavy makeup and seem to respond almost too well to your overtures. They're probably prostitutes.

When an Apology Is in Order

We've all had the experience of seeing a beautiful stranger across a crowded room. You're supposed to be concentrating on a lecture or presentation but all you can do is gaze at and wonder about the beautiful stranger. She probably realizes you've been staring. This gives you the perfect excuse to start a conversation.

Go up to her and say, in the most heartfelt tones you can muster, "Excuse me, but I owe you an apology."

She, bewildered, will ask, "What for?"

Answer, "For staring at you. I was trying to concentrate on the lecture but I found myself just gazing at you the whole time." Shrug helplessly and say, "I'm sorry, but my eyes just seemed to have a will of their own."

Ask if there's any way you can make up for your rudeness; if she says that's okay and looks away quickly, she's not fertile ground. If she laughs and looks at you measuringly, plow ahead.

To some people, love means never having to say you're sorry. To others, saying you're sorry is one way to get love.

Getting Her up to Your Apartment

Beg, coax, wheedle, and cajole, but the best way to get her up to your apartment is a straightforward lie: "Come on up to my apartment. I *promise* I won't make a pass at you." After you make a pass, when she calls you on your promise, just shrug and admit you lied.

Or try, "Come up to my apartment. I *know* you won't go to bed with me. I just want to be *with* you a little while longer." This will ease her worries about being attacked. Second, she'll be relieved to know that you don't perceive her as "that" type of woman, which seems to be every woman's worst fear. (Once she's reassured you don't think of her that way, she'll be more willing to *be* that way.)

Tell her your roommates are having a party tonight, and ask her to stop by for a while. When she wonders where everybody else is, shrug and say, "I guess the party's just you and me."

Or sweeten the bait. Tell her you have an original Picasso. This approach is like that of the fellow who would tell women he had a nine-inch member: By the time they found out how gross his exaggerations were, he'd already gotten what he wanted.

Getting Her out of Your Apartment

Q: What's the definition of a Cinderella 10?
A: A woman who sucks and screws until midnight and then turns into a pizza and beer.

—Anonymous

Before sex a woman is the most desirable thing in the world. After sex she can seem like the most undesirable. How do you kick her out of your pad without seeming to do so?

Say, "I have to pick up my pit bull at the vet's in an hour. Wanna come?"

Ask if she'd like to shoot some heroin. (If she says yes, you're the one in trouble.)

Close all the windows and pull the shades, saying there's somebody who wants to kill you and you're afraid he may try to shoot you through the window. (Whether she believes you or not, she'll want to get away.)

Admit you're bisexual.

Say, "Oh, Christ, my wife is due back in half an hour!" (Substitute "girlfriend" for "wife" if you're under twenty-two.)

Mention that you were just released from a mental institution. ("I'm okay now. My violence is in the past.")

Repeatedly break wind loudly and laugh hysterically every time.

Blow your nose on your shirt.

When you're sated with sex and the ball game on TV beckons, there's no need to put up with pesky annoyances.

Getting into Her Apartment

You've taken your target out on an expensive date, and you're escorting her home. You don't want to settle for "Thanks for a wonderful evening" and a peck on the cheek at her front door. To avoid this humiliation, you must plot your campaign with great care beforehand.

Bring along a heavy book when you pick her up for the date. Naturally, you'll want to leave it at her place rather than have to lug it around on the date. Afterward, you'll have an excuse to go up to her room.

If you don't have a bulky book handy, or if you didn't pick her up at her place, there's another method. When you're walking her back to her place (there are so many muggers around these days), mention that you have to take a leak. Jokingly ask if she'd mind if you did it there on the street. She'll probably express dismay at your lack of manners. So be a gentleman and wait. That way, when you get to her door and ask if you can use her bathroom, she can hardly refuse.

Getting into her apartment is, of course, no guarantee of scoring. But being kept out is a sure guarantee that you won't.

Keep from Getting Kicked Out of Her Apartment

To penetrate the inner sanctum, one must first keep from getting thrown out of the fortress. This can require both tenacity and cunning.

When one has been particularly insistent in one's attempts at seduction, women have a disturbingly uniform tendency to say, "You'd better leave now." You must keep the referee (she holds that position) from ejecting you from the game.

Say you've misplaced the key to your apartment and must wait for your roommate to return before you can go home. Sporadically make bogus phone calls home and express exasperation at your roommate's tardiness.

Or make a bogus call for a taxi and wait for it to arrive. (Taxis never arrive on time.) Women may let their guard down about sex play if they think they will be saved by the bell before the act can be consummated.

If your car is at her place, pretend it won't start, then make a bogus call to a towing service.

If you are near a body of water, be it a pool, a lake, or even a fountain, "accidentally" fall in before you get to her place. When you get to her place, you'll have to take your clothes off and dry them out before you leave (she can hardly insist you go home in sopping clothes). This leads to a sexually charged scenario at her apartment (with you having to pad around in a towel or her bathrobe). And you'll have a couple hours' grace before you can be booted.

There's no ignominy in having to leave her apartment. The ignominy is in getting kicked out before you've scored.

Sneaking into Her Roommate's Room After Your Girlfriend Has Fallen Asleep

It's 1:00 A.M. You've just thrown a fuck into your steady girlfriend. She's snoring next to you, the saliva dribbling from her mouth. The idea of putting it to her again is not appealing.

Suddenly it occurs to you that Kathy, her luscious roommate you've always had a yearning for, is in the next room, and she's alone tonight. Making as little noise as possible, you gently ease yourself off the bed and tiptoe to the door. You step into the hallway and close the door behind you.

Then the doubts set in. Will Kathy, out of some misplaced sense of loyalty, deny you the booty? Have no fear. There are ways to overcome her nobler instincts. And if Kathy's attitude remains frosty, you can always pretend you couldn't sleep and just wanted to talk.

If you can find a red ribbon, tie it around your throat. Then, if Kathy is awake when you open the door, hold out your arms and say, "Sally sent me as a present to you."

If she starts to object, say, "Shh! Sally will hear." This tacitly makes her an accomplice before she realizes what's going on. If she still objects, remind her how hurt Sally would be if she discovered the two of you together.

The roommate-visitor has two traditional enemies: creaky floors and squeaky door hinges. It's best to have tested these beforehand, but if you do inadvertently make some noise, freeze for at least a minute. It may take you half an hour to get to Kathy's room, but it is well worth the time.

If, when you get back, your girlfriend asks where you were, say, "The bathroom." If she asks why you were away for such a long time, tell her you were constipated. She can't very well ask you to prove it.

Postcoitus Manners

What's the definition of an eternity?
The time between your orgasm and when she leaves your apartment.

—Anonymous

Postcoitus manners can be divided into two categories: if you want to see the woman again, and if you don't. If it's the latter, do as you please. You can pull your pants on and walk

92

out without a further word; or you can use her bedside phone to call your buddy and tell him you scored.

If you want to see her again, however, such latitude is not yours. A woman whose sexual appeal is marginal to begin with can look downright repellent in the cold postcoital light. But if she tries to kiss you, you can't just push her away. You must conceal your overwhelming desire to get away from her. You must even pretend that she is still desirable. And you can't offend her by showing too much urgency in washing her essence off afterward.

Most women can sense that this is the time when a man's affections are at low tide; a few hugs and kisses now will reassure her that your regard for her is not entirely testicular. And this will assure a return bout when you're again in the mood.

Once nature has taken its course, many guys will mutter hurried excuses about having to get a good night's sleep since they have to get up early to go to work. A less transparent tactic is to pretend to fall asleep on the spot. This effectively cuts off all contact. Feeling drowsy afterward is perfectly natural and it probably won't occur to her that you're faking. She may take this as her cue to leave (if it's your apartment), or fall asleep (if it's hers), in which case you can just leave and tell her later you hadn't wanted to wake her.

Being Cute in Bed

You've just boffed Miss Bimbo and you're in imminent danger of either boredom or disgust, probably both. How to stave them off? Joke around a little.

Immediately after consummating the act, stand up on the bed, raise your arms above your head, thrust your pelvis forward, and yell, "I'm a stuuuuuuuud!" Then place your foot lightly on her torso, beat your chest, and let forth a Tarzan yell.

Ask her, "What tune am I playing?" and pretend to play the piano on her body. Let your hands stray a bit, then add, "I know all the right keys." Or pretend to tap out a message in Morse code onto her body and ask if she can decipher it.

Pretend to wrestle or box with her.

Put a "No Touching" sign on yourself.

Do an imitation of her having an orgasm. (If you're not sure if she had one, just do an imitation of her lovemaking.)

Indicate two spots on her body and say, "You're beautiful from here to here." (Exclude at least half her body.) This should start an interesting conversation.

If she should stand up naked, sink to your knees in front of her and recite the following while holding your right hand over your heart and gazing up at her crotch: "I pledge allegiance to the flag of [her first name] of [her last name], and to the sweet pubics on which it stands, with libertine juices for all."

Pretend to be a dog, sniffing at her areas of greatest olfactory output. Pant with your tongue hanging out and wag an imaginary tail.

After you've initiated the next bout, when she is about to reach her moment of peak ecstasy, stop whatever you're doing and insist you're not going to continue unless she'll do your next batch of laundry.

Keep a book on a bedside stand and then, when you're supposed to be in the mist of rapture, pick it up and start reading it. Even better, keep a "girlie" magazine handy, and then, while going at it, pull it out and open up the centerfold on her stomach (or back).

Just remember that while in bed, she's supposed to laugh with you, not at you.

Excuses for Impotence

It happens to everyone. There are times when, for whatever psychological or physiological reasons, the old heat-seeking missile just refuses to do its duty.

Nonetheless, it's hard for any man to divorce himself from his male ego, and if and when this happens to you, you will undoubtedly feel embarrassed. However, trying to salvage your masculine self-esteem by announcing, "I guess you weren't enough inspiration" or "How do you expect a guy to get excited about a flabby body like that?" is not the right course. Blaming her, while providing you satisfaction of a sort, will dissuade her from becoming intimate later.

Tell her instead you were nervous since you're so taken with her and wanted so badly to impress her: "I've dreamed about this moment so many times, when it finally came, I just felt paralyzed." This bit of reverse psychology should allow for a return engagement. Or, in a slightly bolder vein, "I've masturbated over you so many times, now that I have the real thing, it's just too much for me to handle."

Jokingly lay the blame on a third party. For example, "I'm sorry. It's just that I'm so worried about the economy/the possibility of nuclear war/the Mideast situation," to name three problems you can count on not to defend themselves *or* to disappear.

Whatever you do, reassure the woman it's not because she's unattractive.

Then, if you can pull it off, act perfectly unaffected. Smile and say, "Oh, well. I guess this isn't your lucky day. Can I fix you a drink?" If the woman has ever been with an impotent guy before, she has undoubtedly had the additional misfortune of watching him fall to pieces and then having to spend half her evening consoling him. If you can retain your cool, her overall impression of you may be even better than had you given her a thorough fucking.

Convincing Lies to Tell Your Buddies

As everyone knows, the boasting afterward is the most satisfying part of the mating ritual. Having nothing to boast about is no reason to deny yourself this exquisite pleasure.

Any skilled liar knows that the most effective lies are not outright lies, but mere implications. When your friends eagerly ask, "Didja score?" don't admit anything; just look pleased. (You'll not only get a reputation as a successful womanizer, you'll also be admired for your discretion.)

But if you don't derive enough enjoyment from such subtlety, here are some morning-after lines that have the ring of accomplishment:

1. Uhh . . . ask her.
2. We did it four times last night. Well, actually it was three times in the evening and then once again in the morning.
3. It wasn't any big thrill. I mean, she was just like every other woman. I think it's time for me to settle down.

4. Man, I don't even want to *look* at another woman for at least a week.
5. I was surprised she gave in as quickly as she did. I was expecting more resistance.
6. You know, it was sort of embarrassing, because at first I couldn't even get it up. I redeemed myself later on, though.
7. I was surprised—she looks better in clothes. She really does.
8. I'm glad she let me in the second time, 'cause I came awful quick the first time.
9. She had her period, so I had to cornhole her.

After you've told a lie for a certain length of time, it sort of develops into a fact anyway.

Be sure to claim a failure occasionally, in order to help your credibility. (Nobody always scores.)

Hiding an Affair from Your Wife

There's an expression in athletics that a tie game is like kissing your sister. Well, after a while, being married seems like the game ending in a tie. How do you conceal the occasional win from your wife?

You must do just the opposite of what your instincts compel you to. Most men rush home, blurt out an excuse for their lateness, take a shower, then guiltily lavish their wives with affection (if not with sex). This behavior will immediately raise a wife's suspicions. A gift of diamond earrings or the like will confirm those suspicions. The correct behavior is to be your usual uncommunicative self.

When she asks where you've been, you needn't go to the extreme of saying, "None of your business." Just reply mildly that you had to stay late at the office. (It helps to have a coworker who'll corroborate your story.) Casually comment that it was a pain. If she expresses doubt, snap at her. Immediately apologize, but at least you'll have her on the defensive.

Or, when she asks where you've been, retort that you were just out screwing a luscious eighteen-year-old. Since no husband who was recently unfaithful would have the nerve to reply in this way, her suspicions will be immediately put to rest.

If it's worth staying married, it's worth hiding your affair from your wife. Discretion is definitely the better part of an indiscretion.

If You're Older Than She Is

The older you get, the more attractive younger women there are—and the greater the age difference between you and them. You must be prepared to make light of this to surmount the age barrier.

Start by telling her, "I know I'm not young and pretty anymore, but"—shrug modestly here—"I make up for that by being old and ugly."

If you are less than thirty-four, tell her, "I feel a midlife crisis coming on. I need an affair with a younger woman." Add: "I think it would be a learning experience for you to have sex with an older man—just so you could see how little you have to look forward to."

Put her at ease by claiming that at the ripe old age of thirty-four, you're not much troubled by a sex drive anymore, therefore you're not a threat to her. (Even if you're twenty-four to her eighteen, you'll seem old to her. And all women have heard that a man reaches his sexual peak at seventeen.)

Say, "Really, it's quite a relief. Having a strong sex drive just makes you act silly. Now, I can relax and be myself. I'm telling you, for me, sex is just a not-so-fond memory." Add: "At my age, I don't need sex more than once a month, and I just had it last week, so I'm . . . harmless."

If you want to play it a little more romantic, say, "I thought I was too old to have crushes anymore, but here I am at the age of fifty-two with this ridiculous schoolboy crush on you." Shake your head disgustedly and say, "I'm pathetic."

Do resist the temptation to say, "I was young once, too, you know." This really will make you sound old.

Remember, you're only as old as she feels you are.

Throw Her a Bachelorette Party

A woman you've taken a fancy to is about to get married. The invitations have been mailed, the wedding gown selected, the photographer and limousine hired. It's too late to stop it. But it's not too late for a final trip to her altar.

You should weave the following into your conversation with the bride-to-be.

"So, is anyone throwing you a bachelorette party?"

"I had a bridal shower. Is that the same thing?"

"No. I mean a bachelorette party, like the bachelor party he's gonna get."

"I don't think so."

"But you *have* to have a bachelorette party. One last drunken blowout and fling before a lifetime of married boredom."

"What do you mean, 'fling'?"

"Well, it's only fair. He's gonna have one at the bachelor party. They always hire some whore to blow the groom. It's a custom."

"What?!"

"Yeah, it's a custom. Guys keep it secret, but it always happens. If the groom didn't go through with it everybody would call him a wimp."

"Oh, no. You're kidding, right?"

"No. I tell you what. If they're not throwing you a party, I'll throw you one."

Tell her the party starts off with some drinks at your apartment, to get in the mood. After a few drinks, ask her if he was her first choice for a husband. Then ask if she thinks she was his first choice. Both questions should put things in perspective, and the second should strike a nice, deep chord of insecurity, the kind that drives people to act rashly.

If you've had enough to drink, and if you feel you can pull it off, put on some music and do a striptease for her, always clowning just a bit to let her know it's all in jest. (You may need more than a few drinks for this.) Emphasize that after her marriage she'll only have one man for the rest of her entire life. She may find this thought as depressing as you would.

With enough persuasion, you'll be able to give her the wedding present of *your* choice and ensure she has reason to be a blushing bride.

The Blind Date

We've all been told about some wonderful woman we just have to meet. But since the matchmaker almost never has her photo, we've no idea what she looks like. As often as not, she turns out to look as if her plastic surgeon put the silicone in the wrong places. But this isn't always true, so don't turn down a blind date on principle.

In fact, arrange a date. Then buy some flowers, call her ten minutes before you're supposed to meet, and say you're really sorry but that an emergency came up (make it plausible) and you won't be able to go out, but you wanted to drop some flowers off by way of apology. Stress that you want to get together another time. She should be as curious to see you as you are to see her, and her anger should be mollified by the flowers, so she'll probably agree to let you stop by. If she turns out to be a bow-wow, give her the flowers, apologize profusely, make vague plans for the future, and exit as planned.

If you find her attractive, have this speech ready: "I have a confession. I've had blind dates in the past with two girls; both were unattractive. I thought you'd probably be the same, so that's why I decided to back out at the last minute. But now that I've seen how beautiful you are, I'd really like to take you out, if that's still an option." She probably won't have made plans in the ten minutes since you've phoned, and since she'll probably be flattered (even if she disapproves of your tactics), she'll probably say yes.

Just remember that when she answers the door, you must make your decision instantaneously. If you hem and haw while trying to decide if you want to go out with her, she'll realize something is amiss.

The Movie Date

A movie is a great place to bring a boring girl, as it will free you from her conversation for two hours. But while effectively shutting off contact may provide welcome relief, there are ways to amuse your date sporadically and maintain the pretense of social intercourse during the screening.

The one way not to do this is, if you've already seen the movie, to tell her what happens next. There's no better way to ruin a movie.

But do talk occasionally. Lean in close and whisper something innocuous. Five seconds later lean in again and whisper, "The only reason I said that was so I could put my face close to yours." (Wait a few seconds before you move away.)

When the hero first appears, whisper, "That's what I want to look like when I grow up."

Whenever the hero kisses the heroine, try to kiss your date. Eventually whenever two people kiss on screen, all you'll have to do is look at her and she'll start giggling.

If it's a scary movie, start repeating to yourself in a low voice, "It's only a movie. . . . It's only a movie. . . ." Or bury your head in her shoulder and whisper, "Tell me when it's over." Afterward, ask her if she was scared; insist you weren't.

If the movie's lousy, look at her and hold your nose. If you know she felt the same way, stand up after it's over and clap loudly, proclaiming, "Wonderful movie."

When you emerge from the theater, you'll both feel dazed and slightly discombobulated, as if you're coming out of a long hibernation. In this state, she is relatively defenseless; this is a good time to suggest something she might not otherwise be amenable to, like a nightcap at your apartment.

Take advantage of all these opportunities, and the movie will more likely have a happy ending for you.

Cheap Thrills

Psychological studies have shown that when people experience a strong physical sensation, they will associate their heightened feeling with whomever they are with at the time. If you are present when your target has that experience, she will imprint on you. And fear makes people want to have sex. It's why more babies are conceived in wartime.

When two people step off a roller coaster ride, they have a number of heady feelings. They are relieved to be back on solid ground, giddy from the ride, and still tingling from the adrenaline jolt. They are proud of their bravery, and drawn closer by their shared experience. What's more, having been on an exciting roller coaster ride together, each will associate that feeling of excitement with the other. They also will feel a compulsion to duplicate those tingles with other physical thrills.

Your mutual adventure needn't necessarily be a roller coaster ride. Take her swimming in fifty-five-degree water and she'll associate that exhilarating, breathtaking, nipple-tightening sensation with you. Take your target skydiving.

If she's athletic, take her running to exhaustion. The endorphins (the body's natural painkillers) will give her a natural high, and her muscles may be sore enough afterward to require a massage.

Take her snow- or water-skiing, depending on the season and your locale. Or just have a snowball fight or a water balloon fight. Hang-glide, wind-surf, do anything that will stimulate her heart rate and get her juices flowing.

Once her heart rate has topped 120, once the adrenal iceman has stuck his fingers into her stomach, she's not going to be in the mood for a quiet evening curled around a book. After some exhilarating chills and spills, what she wants is action, which is what you are there to provide.

It's a cheap trick, but it works.

The Natural History Museum Date

This is a fun place to spend an afternoon, all the more so with a travelogue designed to amuse both yourself and your target.

There is plenty to talk about. If there is a tableau of Native Americans, say, "That was me in another life. But I killed too many enemy warriors and my punishment was to be reincarnated as a luckless fellow who would fall hopelessly in love with a woman who wouldn't sleep with him."

If the women in the exhibits are wearing revealing costumes, comment, "You'd look quite fetching in that outfit."

If one of the scenes depicts life in the Stone Age, nod

judiciously and muse, "Those were the days a man could just club a woman and drag her off to his cave."

When you get to the animal section, show off your knowledge of zoology. At the hippopotamus exhibit, say, "Man, that is one fat rhino!" At the zebra display, exclaim, "Wow! Striped horses!"

If you see an eland, with its penis extending halfway up its belly, wonder out loud, "Can you imagine having one that small?"

If you see an exhibit of an elk being attacked by a pack of snarling wolves, say, "That's what I felt like when I met your family," or, if more appropriate, "That's going to be you when you meet my family."

Show off your knowledge of evolution as you pass the displays. "The jackrabbits grew such big ears because they were always afraid the other jackrabbits were talking about them. . . . The leopard grew spots because they were vain and wanted their furs to be more valuable."

Expound on the mating habits of the various animals. ("If the male lion is horny enough he'll mate with a leopard and if he's really horny he'll even do a wildebeest.") If you actually know something about zoology or evolution, don't be afraid to speak up.

Natural history museums tend to be great places to play touchy-feely with your target. There are lots of dark corners and deserted hallways that are just tailor-made for fooling around. The fact that you obviously can't go all the way there prevents her from getting too defensive, and she may just get hot and bothered enough so that when you eventually get her home, she'll be ready to demonstrate the mating habits of the North American *Hetero sapien*.

Standing Her Up

If you stand your date up, and you want to see her again, you must have a good explanation handy.

Most habitual liars use the impossible-to-disprove excuse; as a result, it is less believable. The traffic jam, for instance, is more than a little dog-eared.

The firm denial works better. ("*I* was there. Where were *you*?") This leaves the resolution of the impossibility up to her. If she contradicts you, which she will at first, insist you were there. Get angry. It's amazing how many women will end up making your excuse for you. ("Oh. You were probably at the other gate.")

Or alter the circumstances of your plans to meet: If you were supposed to meet at six, insist it was seven. Pretend to be as mad as she is. (Method acting is in order.)

Basically, if she likes you, almost any excuse will do (except "I just didn't feel like seeing you").

A Fight Can Be Good Therapy

Love life dull?

Everyone knows that a good fight clears the air, and that after the makeup and mutual self-recriminations, the love-making is better than ever. Here are some good ways to start a fight.

"No offense, but your breath would halt a rhinoceros in full charge."

Look at the floor and say, "What is it, snowing in here?" then look up at her hair and mumble, "Never mind."

"Isn't it about time you had a face-lift?"

To a large-chested woman: "If you don't wear a bra more often, you're going to be playing soccer with those things in a couple of years."

To a small-chested woman: "Did you have a double mastectomy?"

To a dumb woman, after she has proffered evidence of her stupidity: "Have you ever had your IQ tested?"

In general, sarcasm about any sensitive area will suffice. Then, after you've raised her anger to a fever pitch, let her broil for two minutes, turn off the heat, let simmer for ten minutes, then start a tentative apology. She'll accept it as her due. In a few minutes she'll also be contrite—she may have let fly a few nasty insults herself. Then start with the hugs and kisses, and a few minutes later she'll be hot to trot.

Different women have different patterns, but once you've established hers, you can set your clock by it.

Get the Better of a Fight

If you subscribe to the theory that whoever's blood pressure rises less wins the argument, there are several easy ways to better a woman.

One way is calmly to munch on some food while she raves at you. (No one who is furious ever eats.) This will double her outrage.

Pretend to fall asleep while she rages at you. Just say, "Am I tired . . . I'm going to take a little nap now," and pretend to doze off. The veins in her forehead will throb.

Leaf through a magazine while she is steaming at you. Appear absorbed in it, and when she tells you to stop reading and listen to her, continue to read and reply. "I'm listening." She'll hyperventilate.

Laugh and say, "I can't tell whether you're serious." (The spectacle of an angry woman *can* be quite funny.) When she insists she is serious, say with a moan, "You are the most moronic bimbo I've ever met, and that's saying a lot." This is guaranteed to drive her into a frenzy.

Say, "You're cute when you're angry," then look pleased with yourself. The fact that you've made such a banal, un-original comment, then congratulated yourself for your wit, will exacerbate her anger even further.

After she screams at you, calmly look her up and down and ask "Do you want to have sex now?"

As much fun as it is to goad her to new heights of fury, remember that at some point you'll have to coax her back down.

Defusing Her Anger

Women, like alarm clocks, are constitutionally programmed to go off at regular intervals. The difference is that when an alarm clock makes unpleasant noises you merely have to press a button to turn it off.

Some men, blessed with more heart than brains, deal with an angry woman by becoming abjectly apologetic (no matter what the situation mallifying the hellcat at any expense. Other men react by becoming angry (again, no matter what the situation), thereby putting the woman on the defensive. Both techniques work. But there is an easier way.

The first thing to do when she gets angry is to ask, "On a scale of one to ten, how angry are you?" After she says ten or twenty, ask, "If you had a pistol, would you shoot me?" (Don't pop this question if a gun is handy.) After she says yes, ask, "Would you torture me first?" Saying yes will help her vent her anger.

Next, offer to let her hit you on the arm. She probably won't, but if she does, don't worry: Very few women throw a punch that can do any damage (except to their hands). Your willingness to atone with corporal punishment should calm her further.

If she continues to rage, solemnly intone, "Well, at least you're in touch with your emotions. That's healthy." After she castigates you for saying something so stupid, say, "Don't keep them bottled up . . . that's good." After she tells you to shut up, say, "Come on, get madder. You can do better than that!" This will make her tantrum seem absurd and might even make her laugh (which might well make her even angrier). But at least the spell will be broken.

After soothing her, enjoy the peace until it's time for the alarm clock to go clanging off again.

Breaking Up

Every woman knows "I'm not good enough for you" only means "You're not good enough for me." If you want to split, but you're concerned that hell hath no fury, it's much better to get her to break off with you.

One way to get her to do it is to say, "Damn, my herpes is acting up again." Sit back and watch the relationship rapidly disintegrate.

If she has a different background, use every opportunity to heap abuse on her ethnic group. Sprinkle your speech freely with offensive slurs.

Continually borrow money from her. (Don't pay her back until after she's dropped you.)

Constantly pretend to be drunk at the wheel of your car. (This is fun.)

Step in every dog dropping you see. There are two ways

to do this. One is as if by accident, in which case she'll think you're simply clumsy and despise you for that. The other is gleefully to jump on it, in the manner of a child crushing a sand castle. After every splat, grin widely. If she objects to your behavior, act as if she's a bore, and continue anyway. (If she decides to join you, breaking up will be all that much easier.)

If you don't want to dirty your shoes, take a stick and prod at every dog dropping you see. Claim you have an interest in veterinary medicine. ("Hmm, that dog has an iron deficiency.") Then use the stick as a conductor's baton, punctuating your conversational points as you walk along.

That old song to the contrary, breaking up is easy to do.

Answers to Common Excuses

When pressed, many women will often voice one of these universal themes as if they are legitimate reasons for withholding the chooch. Here are some verbal counter punches to confuse, bemuse, or simply stun.

But I hardly know you.	I don't know you very well, either. Do I let it bother me?
I'm having my period.	That's great! This is the one time of the month you don't need any protection.

I'm not in the mood.	Let me lick you for two minutes, *then* tell me you're not in the mood.
You're just not my type.	Close your eyes and pretend it's someone else.
But it's our first date.	Don't think of it as our first date. Think of it as our *last* date.
We have such a beautiful friendship, I don't want to ruin it this way.	Are you kidding? This will make it deeper and more meaningful!
But I have a boyfriend.	Don't worry. I wasn't planning on telling him.

There is almost no insurmountable excuse for withholding the booty.

Love

Should the subject of love ever arise, recite the following speech. "Love means different things to different people. Usually it's just infatuation, or sometimes sexual fixation, sometimes even a mild affection. But overall, 'love' is the most overused word in the English language."

"I do know that if someone you really love were to die

you would be absolutely inconsolable for a long, long time, and that a little piece of you would die forever." (This, by the way, is good a definition of love as any.)

Add, "I honestly think some people aren't capable of that kind of love," thereby implying that you are.

This makes you sound like a soulful person with a great capacity for love and raises the possibility in the back of your target's mind that she just might one day be one of those people whose death would render you inconsolable.

Then lighten the mood with, "So, so far I can't honestly tell you that I *love* you, but I do seem to get these feelings around you that I can't quite control." When she asks you what those are, reply perplexedly, "I want to take your clothes off. . . . Is that bad?"

Why Don't You Like Me?

If a woman has rebuffed even your gentlest, most subtle overtures, take the comically direct approach.

Ask, "Why are you so unfriendly to me?" She'll probably reply, "I'm not that unfriendly." Counter with, "Oh, yes you are. If you ever enter the Miss America contest, you're not going to win the Miss Congeniality portion. Don't get me wrong, you'd win the bathing suit portion—at least you'd get my vote—but you'd be dead last in congeniality."

If she insists she is not unfriendly, she will feel obliged to prove it by being friendlier whenever she sees you. Use the opportunity to ingratiate yourself. If she actually tells you why she's unfriendly, use whatever criticism she levels as helpful advice.

114

If you want to make it more awkward for her to rebuff you, phrase the question thusly: "Do I repel you? What is is about me you don't like?" It would take an uncommonly brutal girl to catalog your flaws calmly. If she does respond negatively, she's more likely to say something like "You're obnoxious," that catchall female phrase that in this context translates as "You're too pushy and too blatantly sexual in your approach." Reply contritely, "Sorry. I like you and just wanted to be friends, that's all."

If a crowd is present, and if you can pull it off, ask your target in a tremulous voice brimming with sensitivity, "Evelyn . . . do you like me?" She'll probably be too embarrassed to do anything but laugh in front of the group, so follow up with "*I* like *you*." Let the comment sit for a few seconds.

Another tactic is to say, "I wish you liked me as much as I like you." Admitting you like her makes it very difficult for her not to say she likes you.

By putting your target on the spot you can pressure her either to rethink her attitude, be more friendly, or at least tell you off with a finality that precludes any more wasted time. And time is your most precious resource. Because in the same way that for some people, time is money, for you, time is pussy.

When She Puts an Embargo on the Booty

Withholding of the booty usually happens one to three weeks after it was first surrendered. Men are usually surprised and angered by this tactic. They ought not be.

Think of it from the woman's viewpoint.

Before she gave it up, the man did anything for her, spending money left and right, lavishing all manner of praise, and generally tippytoeing about very carefully. But once nature took its course, the relationship took on a different complexion: He treated her with as much respect and consideration as he gave his pillow. She, naturally enough, resents this.

So, she struck back in the most effective way she knew, claiming, "We have to prove we can be friends first," or some such nonsense. Another common plaint is, "When we do this I develop expectations about our relationship." Both translate as, "Is this all you want me for?"

Unfortunately, the only solution is to go back to tippytoeing about the way you did when you first dated her. The embargo will then be lifted, and normal channels of trade reopened.

Spending the Least Money Possible

Many is the fellow who, after a date, totals up the bill only to find he would have been better off opting for the sure return of a whorehouse.

Luckily, there are dates that won't set you back a week's pay. Here are a few.

Have a picnic. Women inexplicably like them, even if they do involve a long drive, ants in your food, and mosquitoes.

Attend a free concert in the park. Since many others will be doing likewise, your thriftiness won't be obvious.

Go get an ice cream cone. Even if it's inexpensive, it does

constitute self-indulgence, which, after all, is what spending money is all about.

Steer the conversation toward music, and rave about a symphony she's not familiar with. Then suggest she come over to your place to listen to it.

If she's a health nut, suggest a workout together. Going for a run is absolutely free.

Rent a movie for your VCR. Or record a movie, then every time you meet a different woman, ask her over to see it, claiming you haven't seen it yet.

If you do go out to dinner, ask if she is a feminist. If she says yes, say, "Great, now we can split the cost of dinner."

If your thriftiness has become embarrassingly apparent, it's time for the grandstand gesture. On a night you know your prospect is busy, tell her you bought some tickets to a play and would like her to accompany you. After she reluctantly declines, ask every other woman you know who is busy that night, and get yourself a reputation as a big spender. In that way you won't seem so cheap the next time you suggest a home-cooked dinner.

If you're so stingy you've been jerking off over the same dog-eared skin magazine for the past three years, rest assured you don't need to pay much more to get the real thing.

How to Boast While Seeming Modest

Everyone admires a winner (most women are groupies at heart), but no one likes a boaster. So when you blow your own horn, make it appear accidental.

The subtle boaster knows that one question leads to another. Always refer to an accomplishment seemingly inadvertently in the context of another subject. ("Yeah, broken bones aren't always that painful. . . . After my accident, I didn't know my leg was broken till four hours later.") Let her inquire as to your accident ("I was ski-jumping"), let her inquire as to your involvement in the sport ("Well, I won Nationals once"), then be sure to downplay it ("Ski-jumping isn't big over here the way it is in Europe").

At home, leave mementos of your glory visible, but not stage front and center. Keep the trophies on your mantel, but leave them face down. Count on her to examine them. Place the certificate on the floor where she'll have to step over it. Bury the newspaper clippings in your photo album, but leave the album where she'll spot it (women are congenitally incapable of leaving a photo album unopened).

Talk about a feat she couldn't dream of replicating, then tell her she could do it. ("Breaking boards with your fists just takes a little practice. You could do it.")

Boasting is as deep-seated a need with men as being told they're loved is with women. But as making their need too obvious can render women unattractive, so it can do the same to us.

I'm Too Handsome

Whether you're a one or a ten, you can score modesty points by complaining about how being too good-looking has been such a burden. If you are handsome, she'll think you're making light of your looks. If you're ugly, she'll know you are.

Mournfully mumble, "My problem has always been that I'm just too handsome. Women are intimidated by me. Not to mention that they're afraid they'll look less pretty next to me.

"And women always assume a gorgeous guy is taken, so they never act friendly. Then, when they do, all the time it's the same old line: 'Why don't you become a model?' As if I haven't heard it a million times before."

Cry out in mock agony, "You don't know what a cross this has been to bear. You don't know how many times I've cried myself to sleep at night. . . . I'm considering plastic surgery to make myself more ugly."

Don't go on too long in this vein or she'll think you really are taken with yourself. Always finish with, "Aah, who am I kidding. I know I look like a toad." Then say brightly, "But if you kiss me, I'll turn into a handsome prince."

If she does, and you don't, explain to her that it's a gradual transformation, so she has to keep trying.

When You've Said the Wrong Thing

Gracefully extracting your foot from your mouth is a useful skill in many situations, not the least of which is a date.

When someone has said the wrong thing, he'll often retreat by saying, "Just kidding." This fools no one. Similarly, the overused "I was just testing you" simply means "I was wrong but I don't want to admit it so now I'm making this lame joke."

If you say something dumb, rather than vainly defending your point, simply poke fun at yourself. Before she can contradict you, add, "Can you believe I just said that?"

If you answer an intellectual question in an embarrassingly stupid manner, shrug and say, "Oh, well, I guess the forty grand my parents spent on Princeton was wasted."

If you've said something overpoweringly conceited and the stench of your egotism fills the room, lean forward and say, "That's what we Princeton men call confidence." This will disperse the lingering odor of your comment.

If you've been overly nosy, say, "Much as I hate to pry, that's what I do best."

If you've said something that comes across as too aggressive or overbearing, say, "I just read *Winning Through Intimidation*." Shrug and add, "I read it twice."

With enough practice, you'll make your *faux pas* look intentional, as if you were just setting yourself up for the graceful recoup.

Special Situations

If one of the following occasions arises, have the appropriate response ready.

When you're talking with the guys, you may categorize yourself as a "tit man" or an "ass man." But if the subject comes up and a woman is present, describe yourself as a "brain man." Women always like this (it's hard to figure out why). If the woman has an exceptionally well-formed posterior, however, it won't do any harm to describe yourself as an "ass man." Whatever you do, don't describe yourself as a generic fan of her worst feature.

Should a woman ask, "Why do you like me?" the correct answer is "I don't know. I just do." Many women have been taught that if you answer that you like them for a specific reason, it means your affection is not genuine.

If your target cries out, "Oh, fuck!" in exasperation, reply, "Fuck? I'll do that . . . you'll be disappointed, but at least I'll have a good time."

If she ever tells you that you look sad, shake your head and say, "Every time I've been with a woman recently, it's been the same old story." When she asks for an explanation, her curiosity piqued, reply in tortured tones, "For me to reach my moment of peak ecstasy, I have to close my eyes and pretend it's you." When she laughs, lean close and murmur, "There's only one solution to my problem."

If you're in a restaurant and see a couple of attractive

women waiting to be seated and the hostess is occupied elsewhere, walk up, ask. "Table for two?," then seat them at your table.

When it's time to go off daylight saving time in the fall, tell her, "Listen, I know you have qualms about sleeping with me, but we have to turn the clock back tonight anyway, so why don't you just come over to my apartment at midnight, we'll have some quick fun, then you can go home, we'll turn our clocks back, and it'll be as if it never happened."

Special situations call for special responses.

If Your Reputation Precedes You

If you've been a successful ladies' man in the past, you may acquire a reputation as a womanizer. Since no woman wants to be one in a long line of conquests, that reputation can become self-defeating. So when your latest target flirtatiously says, "I hear you're quite a Romeo," act completely mystified.

Reply, "You know, I've heard that, too, and I have absolutely no idea where I got that reputation. I'm not prolific with women at all. Don't get me wrong—I wish I were. But the fact is, I'm not."

Your target may ask, "Come on, you mean to tell me you didn't have a fling with Susan?" Reply, "No, I swear, we were just friends."

If she asks about other women, unless you dated the

woman in question for months and it's absolutely undeniable, deny it. If she asks about a particularly pretty conquest, reply, "I wish. Janet's beautiful. Not like you, but still beautiful."

If your target believes you, she'll be put off guard and possibly even consider you a challenge. If she doesn't believe you, you get credit for not boasting, and she will worry less that her pubic scalp will be held high in victory.

Basically, what you want to tell your target is the opposite of what you tell the guys.

Part IV

The Target

The Bookworm

Contrary to popular belief, bookish women aren't only attracted to bookish men. What's more, they're particularly unimpressed by men who aspire to but fall short of being cultured. So don't attempt to meet her on her own turf. Pander to her fantasies instead.

Intellectual women always wonder if they're not missing out on "life." So act as if you've just stepped out of a beer commercial, in from a long day of work at the fire station and ready to enjoy some of life's lustier pleasures. *Those* guys obviously don't miss out on "life."

Watching beer commercials on TV is probably as close as she's ever gotten to healthy, guilt-free, blue-collar masculinity (it may be as close as anyone's gotten), so don't worry about being transparent. She probably secretly feels that those lumberjacks who daily celebrate "Miller time" are a more appealing breed than the wimpy eggheads she's accustomed to.

If you deliberately appear less educated than you are, she may find you exotic. If she asks if you've read a certain book, always reply, "No, but I saw the movie." Tell her you've never been out of your home state (any member of the intelligentsia will find this fascinating). And even if you only drink sherry and an occasional brandy snifter, when you're with her drink domestic beer (and never light beer).

If you're having trouble extracting the final thrill from her, pander to her fears. She'll undoubtedly have read a lot of psychology at some point, so remind her, "They say it's unhealthy not to have sex—you'll go crazy." (Young intellectuals often worry about that.)

To seduce the bookworm, use your brawn, not your brains.

The Jockette

She's healthy, she's fit, and she's probably got a trim, appealing figure. She's also proud of her ability in her sport; this is the key to how you seduce her.

Let's assume she's a tennis player. The easiest date to get with her in the first place is a tennis date. Even if you are a far superior tennis player, make sure the match is close. A close match will get her competitive juices flowing (which in turn will stimulate the other kind).

If you crush her, she'll be embarrassed and humiliated—hardly the proper frame of mind for romance. And you will only exacerbate the situation by making comments like, "I thought you said you were good" or "Are you sure this was your sport?" (Although one must admit the pleasure derived from making these comments is often commensurate with the pleasure of a love match.)

If you let her crush you, she will lose respect for you. (This also is not conducive to romance.) So if you're outmatched, pick another sport in which to challenge her.

One stratagem, if you are overwhelmingly better in the

game at hand, is to pretend to make the competition close, but do so in such an obvious manner that she cannot but notice the pretense. You'll not only score points for being nice, she'll admire your athletic prowess as well. However, if her athletic ego is on the line (and you'd be surprised how often it is), it's better not to be too obvious.

If you have been having a drawn-out courtship on the court (or elsewhere), when you are ready to go for the kill, let her win the last game. Being aglow with the thrill of victory will put her in the mood for other thills.

The Virgin

An oft-heard truism is that a woman's first experience with sex is usually a great disappointment. This is often simply because her expectations were too high. A woman as yet uninitiated has heard many times that sex is the ultimate thrill. So, when she eventually tries it, reality almost invariably disappoints. (From that point, it will gradually grow into an acquired taste for her.)

The key to having your way with a virgin is to inflate her expectations even further. Promise her that sex is pleasurable beyond her wildest dreams. Promise that she'll feel the earth move. Promise a once-in-a-lifetime experience (at this stage she can hardly argue that point).

At the same time, a virgin will naturally also have misapprehensions about intercourse. One is that the first time will be painful. (It may be.) Another is that she might not be "good in bed." (Every woman is good as long as she's lubricated and willing.) Another fear is that there will be all sorts of blood when she has sex for the first time. (There may or may not be.) Another is pregnancy. (This should be one of your fears as well.) Another is that she will somehow become addicted to sex. (This is ridiculous.) Reassure her about all these fears except the last.

Once she gives in, she may be disappointed. So what? You won't be.

Adding a cherry to your list is a much more glorious achievement than scoring with another mattressback.

The Beauty

Beauties can be divided into two categories: those who know it and those who don't. A surprising number don't know it, especially the younger ones. (As a rule, men tend to think themselves a little better looking than they are, women a little worse.)

If your target is unaware of her beauty, and a bit insecure, tell her how gorgeous she is. It won't be the first time she's heard it, but rest assured she'll lap it up anyway.

If the woman is aware of her attractiveness, you're in for a hard time because she expects the world on a platter (for good reason, as she usually gets it that way). Her Achilles' heel is that she has probably developed a complex about people liking her for her looks and not for herself (again, for good reason). This is the crux of your game with her.

Whatever you do, don't compliment her on her beauty. Pretend you don't find her attractive in the least, and act accordingly: friendly, but not overwhelmingly attentive. She is used to men fawning all over her, and is not only inured to the flattery but may even find it irritating.

At the same time you play down her looks, however, be sure to flatter her wit, intelligence, and other attributes. This will reassure her that you appreciate her for herself, unlike all those other superficial men. She'll undoubtedly find you a refreshing change.

If the subject of her appearance does come up, tell her, "You know, I find it a bit mystifying that everyone else seems to think you're so good-looking. Don't get me wrong—I think you're perfectly nice-looking. But personally, I just don't see you as beautiful."

Pretend you admire her mind, and she'll reward you with her body.

The Aging Beauty

Any compliments on her beauty will work wonders with this creature (except "You must have been really beautiful ten years ago" or "You look really good for your age").

If you can do so subtly, convey that you think she's younger than she is. ("Do you live with your parents?" or "Do you go to school near here?") If you're substantially younger than she is, describe a third party by saying, "He's about our age." If you're her age, flirtatiously ask if she's ever dated an older man before. Act astonished if she tells you her age (*not* by saying, "Is that all?").

If you refer to a historic event of more than a decade ago, preface it by saying, "You're too young to remember, but . . ."

Whatever you do, don't tell her she's young at heart.

These days many females are hypersensitive about being called a "girl" rather than a "woman"; the aging beauty is not. Comparing her favorably with young beauties is also helpful.

After enough flattery, the aging beauty may acquiesce out of sheer gratitude.

Your Best Friend's Girlfriend

This very sensitive situation must be handled with the utmost delicacy and tact.

The best approach with your buddy's girlfriend (who has probably begun to think of you as a friend) is simply to say that you hate to have to tell her, Joe being the good buddy that he is, but you just can't stand to sit by and watch her being made a fool of while Joe cheats on her with every woman in town—a fact that only she seems to be unaware of.

She will not only lose whatever motivation she had to remain faithful to him, she'll also want to take revenge by cheating on Joe with the nearest guy available, and, well, there you are.

After the two of you are finished, tell her that you were

only kidding about Joe, that he has in fact been faithful to her, and that you're surprised she took you seriously. You'll get hysterics, rage, and recriminations, but you can weather the storm securely with the knowledge that this should effectively prevent her from telling Joe what you've done.

Your Girlfriend's Best Friend

If you used to find Susan and Janet equally attractive, after you've scored with Susan, Janet will undoubtedly seem the more desirable of the two.

But Janet, as Susan's good friend, will probably consider you off-limits. So instead of asking her out, tell her you want to see her to talk about Susan.

When you get together, tell Janet you think Susan's being unfaithful. When Janet asks why you're suspicious, say a man has answered Susan's phone twice. (Be prepared for unwelcome news if Janet confirms your "suspicions.") Next tell her you've decided to be faithful to Susan anyway. Let Janet be the one to suggest you're doing yourself an injustice.

Then steer the conversation to their friendship. "At first I thought you two were such good friends. But Susan is such a backstabber."

"What does she say about me?"

"Oh, I shouldn't say."

"Come on, tell me."

"I shouldn't."

"Come on, you can't just say that and then not tell me."

133

"Well, for one thing she says she thinks you might be a lesbian."

One pleasing aspect of this scenario is that Janet, in her efforts to prove a normal sexuality, should provide a particularly energetic performance.

The Divorced Mother

Every divorced mother thinks her child makes her a less desirable mate in the eyes of a new man. (Usually she's right.) So she is hypersensitive to the way you react to her child.

Soothe her insecurities. Act as if her kid is the most adorable child in the world. *All* women think their child is beautiful, so no matter how ugly the child is, compliment his or her beauty.

Talking to a child is easier than it seems. Just talk about the child's interests—do not fear, he or she will let you know what those are. Play with the child, make him or her laugh, buy the child ice cream. Mommy will glow.

Insist that the child come along on your first date. You'll get off cheaper this way (you can't take a five-year-old to an expensive restaurant). You'll also tire the child out and make the child feel that he or she has had enough attention, so that when the time comes for making a pass at Mommy, the kid will have long since trundled sleepily and willingly off to bed.

You'll also leave Mommy feeling so good about having

indulged Junior that she'll feel like indulging herself later that night.

The Married Woman

We've all read fairy tales that end with the prince and princess marrying and living happily ever after. With apologies to the Brothers Grimm, fairy tales are exactly what these stories are.

Married women are one of the best sources of poontang, if only because there's only one other guy to compete with, and he's usually not that attentive. Most men consider a wedding band off-limits; this sets the stage for you.

Don't try to bed a married woman by questioning her husband's fidelity. Most wives have a pretty good idea whether their husband cheats. If her husband is a philanderer, she knows it already and it will do little good to belabor the point. If he's faithful, bringing up the subject will just make her feel guilty.

Instead, simply say, "If you weren't already married, I'd ask you to marry me." This will make her curious as to what she missed. It will also strike a wistful chord, and for many women, sentiment is a stepping-stone to horniness.

If the married woman expresses dismay at your advances, sing the womanizer's constant refrain: "I thought you *wanted* me to." If this causes further protestation, plead, "You don't know how many times I've insulted women by not trying anything."

The best thing about the married woman is that she doesn't expect a lot of your time, she doesn't expect expensive gifts, and she doesn't expect you to make a commitment—she only expects you to screw her.

The Recent Widow

You'd have to be awfully slimy to attempt this, but if you've read the book this far, you probably qualify, so here's a good tactic for you.

The recently bereaved wife is at her most vulnerable. She is emotionally open. She needs consoling. She feels a universal kinship with her fellow beings, which is kept buried most of the time. And she feels a certain soulfulness that overrides the usual feeling of distrust and suspicion.

When you express your condolences, profess your love for the dear departed, whatever your actual feelings were. Let her know that you share her grief and sense of loss. Be sure to add that her husband would have wanted her to be happy.

It is natural to give her a hug. It is natural to let that hug go on for an extended period. It is natural to hold her hand as a gesture of consolation. Any sort of physical contact will be interpreted as a physical manifestation of your emotional support.

It is also natural for feelings of lust to overcome a man and a woman who are in close physical contact for any length of time, no matter what the circumstances. Let your hug turn into a kiss, then rest your head on her shoulder. Shake your head mournfully and mumble, "I don't know what's wrong with me, this is really horrible, but I want to make love to you. . . . I can't believe I feel this way at a time like this. I'm sorry." With her emotions at a fever pitch, unable to stand her grief, she may just take distraction where she can.

If your conscience starts to bother you, as indeed it should, you can tell yourself as you slither away that at least you made her feel better temporarily.

Stewardesses and Cocktail Waitresses

What do you think of these? Easy sex? So does everyone else. Therein lies the problem. With a reputation like that to live down, these poor women are constantly trying to prove they're not what you think. The biggest mistake you can make is to communicate, consciously or otherwise, that you take their favors for granted.

So don't leer, don't make suggestive comments, and don't talk down to them. The classic wisdom is correct: "Treat a lady like a tramp and a tramp like a lady." (Not that these ladies are tramps, merely that their occupations have that certain aura about them.)

This holds particularly true for the girl your buddy has already had. Saying, "Come on, you let Bernie, why won't you let me?" will only outrage her. (Bernie will be pretty mad, too.)

Do everything short of calling her "Your Highness." Light

her cigarettes, open the door for her, offer her your jacket if it's cold out, and let unctuousness drip from your every word. Roll out the red carpet, and she may just lie down on it.

The Gold-Digger

The gold-digger is the womanizer's mirror image: instead of using money to get sex, she does the opposite. Gold-diggers include just about every good-looking wife or mistress of an unattractive rich man.

However, just because their souls are rotten doesn't mean their bodies aren't heavenly. So play their game. It's not hard to pretend you're rich.

Pretend you're shopping for a country house. Bring your date along as you look at different properties. (Looking at houses may sound boring to you, but it's the type of activity a gold-digger thrives on.) As long as you ask the realtor intelligent questions, he'll think you're seriously in the market. Your date will be convinced you're rich, and you won't have to spend a penny.

Or ask your target to go gallery-hopping. This will leave her with the proper impression. (Only people with money to burn buy art.) Pretend to come close to buying a couple of pieces, but at the last minute find something wrong with each.

"I lost twenty thousand in the market today" will perk up the ears of any gold-digger. She may try to console you in the way she knows best.

If you see her for any length of time, you do eventually have to spend some money. You can fend her off temporarily with, "How come you're always trying to get money out of me? I thought you liked me for *me*." This should shame her into holding off for a little while, but gold-diggers are essentially shameless creatures, and she'll revert to form soon enough.

With the gold-digger, the question you must ask yourself is this: Is the screwing I'm getting worth the screwing I'm getting?

The Social Climber

She goes to parties for the pleasure of turning down all the guys who ask her to dance. (This makes her feel desirable.)

She'll climb all over herself trying to get into the trendiest nightclub, not so she can meet guys, but so she can make the Scene.

It's hard to hold her attention in a conversation because she is constantly distracted by what's happening on the other side of the room.

Her interests are fashion, money, and celebrities. She is first cousin to the gold-digger.

It's easy to be fooled by her because she does love to flirt. In fact, this is her favorite form of sex. She'll talk about guys she'd love to rape but her actions don't speak nearly as loudly as her words.

On a date, she prefers to stay out till all hours of the night rather than going home and getting it.

She would rather be gossiping with her friends than be giving her friends something to gossip about.

Her Achilles' heel is that she's a star-fucker. If you can convince her that you're a star of some kind (sports stars don't count unless they make a lot of money), you have a chance. Otherwise, it's best simply to avoid her. And once you get to know her, there's no doubt about her identity.

The cardinal rule of womanizing is: You can't trust a woman who doesn't like sex.

Dumbbellina

She doesn't know anything about politics, she doesn't know anything about sports, and she doesn't know anything about business. But she always seems to know that you want her only for sex.

Unfortunately, her primary basis for self-respect seems to be that she won't sleep with you immediately. First, you must show that you respect her. Pathetic as this sounds, it's the truth, and it is unwise to ignore her needs.

So every time she opens her mouth, look at her with open admiration and say, "That's really smart." She'll probably believe you. (Whatever you do, don't ever call her stupid.)

Resist the temptation to correct her if she makes errors. And don't try to argue broad philosophical or political issues with her. Steer the conversation toward innocuous topics, such as her favorite foods and places she's been.

She's the perfect candidate for a movie date.

Few things are more obnoxious than the dumb woman who is loudly opinionated, and you'll be encouraging her in this direction with your respect. But if you play your cards right, you can manage a fairly swift screw and an even swifter getaway.

People who don't command respect often demand it, and the less they deserve it, the louder their demands. If the person happens to be a woman whose body you crave, you must pay lip service to her demands before she will pay lip service to you.

Women from the Office

Despite coworkers who caution with such worldly admonitions as "Don't piss where you eat," the office is a great source of poontang. The only dynamic you must battle is that every career woman's biggest fear is that people will regard her primarily as a piece of ass and only secondarily as a professional.

To surmount this obstacle, you must pretend that this is your biggest fear as well. So when you ask Ms. Coworker out for a drink after work, insist she not tell anyone. In this way she'll regard you as a coconspirator, not a potential informant. When the possibility of an affair arises, swear her to secrecy (because you don't want to jeopardize your career). Convince her you have the same vested interest.

If the woman is a professional, or sees herself as one, drop a few lines about how hard it is for women to get ahead in your business. (Whatever field you're in, you can be fairly sure this is the case.)

If, on the first date, she expresses reluctance to have sex on the grounds that it is only your first date, use the following logic: "Normally, when a man and a woman go out on a first date, they have dinner and see a movie, right? That's a total of about two hours of actual talking and getting to know each other. Well, you and I have seen each other at the office every day for the past year. And each day we've talked about ten minutes. That's about two thousand, five hundred minutes of talking, which is more than forty-one hours, which is the equivalent of twenty dates. Now do you mean to tell me that on our twenty-first date you're *still* not going to come across?"

Just because a fellow can't sleep his way to the top of a corporation doesn't mean he can't enjoy a few of its fringe benefits.

Part V
Obstacles

When One Girlfriend Runs into Another

This ticklish situation calls for an immediate, proactive response.

The one thing you cannot do is act visibly embarrassed, which will ruin your chances with both women. You must brazen it out (assuming the women don't know each other). Turn to the woman you bumped into and introduce the woman you're out with this way: "Becky! I was hoping we would run into you. I want to introduce Sheila, my cousin from Massachusetts. She's down for a few days and I'm showing her around." This should allay Becky's suspicions.

As soon as you've parted company with Becky, turn to Sheila, who will undoubtedly be fuming, and say, "Sheila, please don't take this the wrong way. Becky wanted to go out with me but I turned her down. If she sees me out with another woman it would just be rubbing her face in it. Really. I didn't want to hurt her feelings, that's all." This way, you get credit for kindliness as well as faithfulness.

When you get home call Becky to tell her how happy you are that she got to meet your cousin. Should she express doubt regarding your blood ties to Sheila (especially if Sheila shot you a killing look at the time), scoff at her suspicions. "Come on! Do you think I'd ever actually introduce some woman I was on a date with as my cousin? What kind of woman would put up with that kind of slap in the face?

And what kind of guy do you think I am to do that to a woman?"

If she answers this last question spitefully, act hurt. "Becky . . . do you really think I'm like that?" If she answers affirmatively, get angry. ("I'm really insulted. I'm not sure I want to see you anymore.") This should cause her to backpedal.

Don't act mollified. After all, she has a hell of a lot of nerve accusing you of being such a sleazeball.

When She Has a Boyfriend

If a woman hides behind the old excuse "I have a boyfriend," keep pressing the attack.

Immediately reply, "I know *lots* of women who have enough love in their hearts for *two* boyfriends." If she looks hesitant, ask, "Is your boyfriend the jealous type?" She'll probably say "Yes," to which the proper response is, "Is he big?"

Ask where he lives. If he lives far away, say, "That's not a boyfriend. That's a pen pal."

Ask, "What's his address?" When she replies "Why?" tell her you've decided to kill him. (Make sure she knows you're kidding.)

Explain to the woman that she ought to date you just to make the boyfriend jealous. After all, a jealous boyfriend is an attentive boyfriend, and there's nothing that will make him more attentive than being kept in a constant state of insecurity. As, "Is he taking you for granted? You ought to teach that bastard a lesson." Explain that jealousy is just the right stimulant for a flagging relationship.

If she still refuses to see you, accuse her of not caring about her boyfriend.

If She Is Still Recalcitrant

If you continue to pursue an uncooperative subject, it's best to do so in a joking manner that will keep her too amused to be angry.

When she doesn't respond to your suggestions, cry out, "You keep missing your cues! Now let's take that scene again."

If you have any unique qualities, play on them: "This is probably the last chance in your entire life to make it with a guy named Casanova."

Tell her, "You can't reject me. These are my formative years. This could be a traumatic experience for me."

If she complains about anything at all in her life that has gone wrong, nod your head knowingly. "See? That's what happens if you don't go out with me."

If she remains unmoved, ask, "Do you have a heart?" When she says "Yes," ask, "Is it made of stone?"

If she spells out the fact that she doesn't like you at all, in fact can't stand you, reply reprovingly, "You—you won't even let a guy *dream*, will you?"

Eventually your target may surrender through sheer exhaustion.

If you feel you've come on too strong, you can lighten up your final impression with, "Well, I hope you didn't feel too much like Jodie Foster to my John Hinckley."

Turn Rejection into an Opportunity

Many guys, upon being rebuffed, become antagonistic. But burning your bridges is a silly mistake. This is the best time to show that you are good-hearted, sincere, and secure enough to suffer rejection calmly. Also, once a woman has turned you down, she feels she can lower her guard, and you can then make headway.

If she tells you she's unavailable, just say, "Well, I'm sorry to hear that. For whatever it's worth to you, I really do have an *insane* crush on you." Draw out the word "insane."

If she claims to feel bad about hurting your feelings, reply, "You don't have to feel bad—I've had lots of experience being rejected by women." This establishes just the right tone of modesty and humor. Then claim, "You're not missing much anyway: I'm just your average guy—three parts conceit and two parts insecurity." (No average guy would say this.)

If she suggests you should have no problem finding someone else, reply, "It's hard to get excited over a Big Mac once you've seen filet mignon."

Later, ask, "Can you tell just by looking at me that my heart is broken?" She'll probably laugh and deny it. Mournfully mumble, "I'm going to kill myself."

The next time you see her, say, "I read in a book the other day that when you're trying to get over a crush on someone, you're supposed to imagine them in a ridiculous

148

situation. So recently I've taken to imagining you without any clothes on. That doesn't seem to help at *all*!"

It takes time to seduce women who are currently off-limits, but if you work slowly on ten or twelve at a time, you may later be able to pick them off one by one.

If You've Come Across a Bit Too Strong

We have all at times been overly pushy in a doomed attempt at scoring. In situations like these, there's nothing for it but to eat humble pie and lie like hell about your future intentions.

First apologize for acting "way out of line" and reassure her, "You know me, I'm the type of guy who's all talk and no action anyway." Most women will actually give this line some credibility.

Tell her, "From now on, I want you to think of me as you would one of your gay friends. In fact, think of me as your competition for men." Mince around and overplay it a bit. Then say, "I'm sorry, I have a tendency to turn everything into a joke."

Add, "You're not really my type anyway. In all honesty, you could invite me to your apartment, ask me into your bedroom, take off all your clothes, lie down on your bed, spread your legs and ask me to make love to you, and I'd probably just say thanks but no thanks. That's the truth."

If she expresses disbelief, admit, "Okay, okay, maybe that's not true. But I tell you what: I'm going to cure myself. Every

time I have a lustful thought toward you I'll slap myself."
Hold up a finger and pedantically state, "It's called aversion
therapy. Pretty soon, whenever I see you I'll just wince." At
regular intervals, glance down at her body and then slap
yourself (lightly).

If she still expresses dismay at your aggressiveness, reply,
"Okay, okay, you win. But just think of the status involved:
How many people can say they've got their very own per-
sonal stalker?"

Getting Your Last Digs In

When a woman rejects you, and it's plain you'll have no
future chance with her, you'll likely be momentarily non-
plussed, and the opportune moment may pass before you can
gather your wits to deliver the appropriate farewell. Thus
it's best to have the right insult on file.

The best insult is one tailored specifically to her. Obviously this book cannot determine your target's sensitive
points. But if you're not certain what they are, the following
parting shots should have a nicely deflating effect on her ego.

If you haven't scored with her yet, let her know her only
meaning was as a statistic: "Damn! Joe's still winning the
bet."

"What bet?"

"The one on how many girls each of us screw this year.
He's leading, eight to six. And I thought you were a sure
thing, too."

If she rejects you in person, say, "Wait a sec," then phone another woman and ask for a date. If the other woman doesn't pan out, turn back to the first woman and say, "Come on, go out with me just tonight." (The implication is that she was second choice all along.)

If the woman is terminating a relationship, muse, "I guess from now on when I cheat on you I won't really be cheating anymore."

Pointing out a physical flaw works wonders. ("That blubbery ass didn't do a whole lot for me anyway.")

Dredge up a past trauma of hers and imply that she deserved it.

Say, "I've been meaning to tell you, I tested positive for gonorrhea last week. You better get yourself checked out." (She'll not only worry herself silly, she'll also waste the time and expense of a doctor's appointment.)

Hide your own emotional turmoil as you deliver your parting shot. If you are matter-of-fact about it, the insult will have more bite.

How to Cure a Broken Heart

The first rule of womanizing is: Never fall in love. Should you break that rule and be spurned, you may feel inconsolable.

Well-meaning friends will try to comfort you with such clichés such as, "There are many fish in the sea" or "It was her loss." These are the wrong clichés.

The right cliché ordinarily refers to another ailment: "The best medicine is a hair of the dog that bit you." In other words, jump aboard the first girl you can get your hands on. It is physiologically impossible to suffer from a rock-bottom depression if you have just gotten laid.

If you can't find a willing woman, then go out and get rejected by at least three more women. This will put the initial rejection in perspective. It sounds silly, but it works.

Another distraction is physical pain. Run two miles absolutely all out. The burning of your lungs will make the ache of your heart seem faint by comparison.

If you're susceptible to melancholia, you have undoubtedly been so affected before. Examine your history. Was the last heart-breaker still filling your thoughts three months later? This one won't be, either.

Then again, if you're dumb enough to fall in love, you deserve what you get—so pay no attention to this chapter.

If She Sees This Book on Your Bookshelf

If Machiavelli had had a prince for a disciple, the first thing he would have recommended him to do would have been to write a book against Machiavellianism.
                              —Voltaire (to Frederick the Great of Prussia)

If your target should spot this guide in your apartment, tell her it was a gift and the only reason you haven't thrown it out is you don't want to hurt your friend's feelings: "I guess it was Bill's idea of a sick joke. What gets me is that some borderline perverts out there might actually try stunts like those."

If she says she's read it—and you've already used one of the tactics suggested herein—immediately claim you read only the first few chapters before you stopped in disgust. (If she's read the book and you've used several of the tactics, she won't be in your apartment in the first place.)

If she hasn't read the book and you've used several of the tactics, by all means prevent a casual perusal. If you must, take the book from her and toss it in the toilet, saying, "That's where it belongs." She won't try to retrieve it.

The main thrust of this book is that the less you seem like you'd follow its advice, the greater your chances of success.

Afterword

Normal girls are unable to resist if you exhibit a sense of humor, charm, and a minimal amount of kindness. Even if you're a brazen cad, girls can often be fooled by an act which combines equal parts self-deprecation, wit and flattery. All you really need is the requisite nerve (or perhaps gall) to pull it off. You also want to make her feel very special—as if you don't always chase every girl you fancy. If you read this book you will see exactly how to go about it. Jealousy, gratitude, admiration and other emotions can be manipulated to have just the effect you desire. Novice or expert, you'll undoubtedly chuckle over the most exuberantly risqué tactics you've ever heard. All is fair, as you constantly hear, in love and war. So study up and give yourself an unfair advantage.

About the Author

NICK CASANOVA lives in Manhattan and was single until the age of thirty-one.